Rites of Passage

Christine Hall

Rites of Passage

©2000 Christine Hall

ISBN 186163 086 7

Cover design by Paul Mason

Published by:

Capall Bann Publishing
Freshfields
Chieveley
Berks
RG20 8TF

Acknowledgements

I would like to thank everyone who supported this book project by contributing their thoughts, experiences and encouragement.

Special thanks to the poets who have allowed me to include their poems in this volume: Angela Harrison, Lawrence Long, Linda Vincent, Carol Ann Bill, Kazz and Sarah Rooke.

Also to Natasha Duggan for the illustrations.

Contents

Chapter 1
Celebration and Ritual

Rituals Are For Us

Rituals help us in many ways. They mark special occasions and lend dignity and colour to our events. They comfort and soothe, and give us something purposeful to do. They help us clarify our feelings and needs. They bring us together with other people and they connect as with the spirit world. Best of all, they can be fun and give us joy.

I enjoy celebrating with other people, and I am deeply moved by rituals in which people dedicate part of themselves to a deity, to another person, or to a purpose.

Ignorance about 'what it is all about' is one reason which can spoil people's joy of ritual. The other is that not all rituals are suitable for everyone. Rituals are all around us, and all religions have rituals to mark major occasions.

But these established rituals are not always suitable for everyone. Sometimes they are too solemn for us; sometimes they offend and alienate members of other religions; sometimes they can be inflexible and even hostile. Sometimes a religion doesn't value a phase of life enough to celebrate it with ritual - for example, croning and divorce are ignored by patriarchal religions.

I enjoy organising, devising and conducting rituals. I enjoy participating and assisting in rituals of others of whatever

1

denominations, as long as they are sincere and as long as I am at liberty to withdraw when any aspect of it is uncomfortable.

But I hate rituals in which I have to do things which go against my conscience or nature, or which are just uncomfortable, and I hate to see how some people go through with rituals with which they are clearly not happy.

This is why I have written this book.

How To Use This Book

I want you to enjoy my rituals. I want you to use them, alter them, adjust them, until they are right for you. Since not every word I write can be politically correct in everybody's sense, feel free to turn the words and instructions around, until they feel comfortable to you and your friends.

I assume that most readers follow a Pagan spirituality, in the widest sense, because Paganism is probably the most tolerant of all religions and therefore most suitable to a multi-faith ritual.

I've created my rituals so that they focus on a belief in the Great Mother Goddess who represents nature. If you like, you can substitute the name of a male God, or of several deities, or of Spirits or Guardian Angels or whatever you believe in.

I've assumed that the average reader is female. To write 'he or she', 'his and her' all the time would make the writing clumsy and pompous. Most writers say in their introduction something like 'Sorry ladies, but I'll assume you are all men.' Well, for the sake of balance, I'll assume you're all women. Sorry, gents.

If you don't like this, just replace 'she' by 'he', by 'he/she', by 'it', by 'they' or by whatever is considered politically correct in your circles.

While my rituals are inspired by existing rituals from many cultures and religions, they are not specifically based on any single tradition. If you want a single-faith ritual, your religion will probably have something suitable for you in stock. I have not included any initiation and dedication rituals. These ceremonies with a purely spiritual content are best shared with fellow believers of the same faith. I'm sure your congregation, coven, guild or lodge has its own traditions for these, and can organise a suitable event for you. You won't need my help.

Instead, I've focused on more secular events, for which you don't all have to have the same spiritual ideas.

The order in which the rituals appear in the book is roughly chronological, starting with birth and ending with death. But between those two fixed points everyone's life differs. The events may happen in a different order for you, or not at all.

Planning the Ritual
Many people are hesitating joining in a ritual because they don't know what it is all about. They may be scared to attend a ritual organised by witches or heathens or anyone of a different faith but their own.

'Will they conjure up the devil? Will they sacrifice animals? Will there be dark forces at work? Will I have to take off my clothes? Will I have to participate in a sex orgy? Will my soul be in danger?'

You may smile at those questions. But the fears are real!

The best thing you can do is write an outline of the ritual and give everyone a copy well in advance. This way they can see what is happening, decide whether they are comfortable with it, ask questions about what they don't understand, and accept or decline the invitation.

Having a written outline also allows people to get ready for the event, to choose the right clothes and gifts, and to prepare mentally and spiritually for it, if they wish. It makes conducting the ritual easier, too, because everyone knows what to do when.

Sometimes a person of a strict religion genuinely wants to attend the event, but feels that certain parts of the ritual are conflicting with their conscience. Perhaps they would rather not be present when you invoke the Goddess, or when you look into the crystal ball.

I have always found it easiest to say *'You are very welcome to join just the parts of the ritual you are comfortable with. We'd really like to have you there. Why don't you just slip out when we do [whatever is bothering your friend] and come back when we've finished with it. We'll open the door so you know when to come back in.'*

It is important that they don't feel they are a nuisance when they leave for a while. Give them a smile when they stand up to get out, and smile again when they come back.

If they object to a multi-faith ritual in principle, you can say. 'We are disappointed we can't have you with us during the ritual, but we respect your decision. We hope you'll join us for the party afterwards to celebrate the wedding [the new child, the birthday...]'

Some of my friends are Jehovah's Witnesses, Muslims and members of other strict one-God religions, and by respecting each others' principles and limits we have been able to find enough common ground to share at least some parts of the celebrations together.

But it isn't only religious objections which can be limiting. There may be physical or mental problems. For example, burning incense may be a wonderful mood enhancer, but for some people it can trigger a headache or an asthma attack. If they know about it in advance, they can ask you to refrain from burning incense, or suggest an alternative, or decide to decline the invitation.

Or you may think it marvellously liberating to celebrate skyclad (in the nude) with lots of group huggings. But for your friend who has been repeatedly abused sexually as a child, this would be a terrifying ordeal. Give her the chance to say 'no thank you' rather than confront her with nudity and forced hugs on the day.

Dancing is a wonderful way to celebrate and express joy. But what about those who depend on wheelchairs or crutches? They may feel left out. I like to give them seats in the middle of the room (not in an outside corner!) so that we dance around them, and I encourage them to play a tambourine, a drum or finger cymbals, or to sing, or simply to clap, so that they join with us.

Nudity and All That

Nudity is something wonderful if the occasion is right. But most rituals are not the right occasion. I would certainly decline an invitation to celebrate in the nude. To start with, I'd be shivering with cold. It's all right for you hot blooded creatures, but I'm one of those people who have to wear woollen socks in bed for ten months of the year. Icy toes and blue fingers don't put me in a joyous mood. And there are others out there who'd be equally goose pimpled.

I find dressing up is much more fun than undressing. Choosing clothes for a special occasion and adorning ourselves with make-up and jewellery, is a great way of preparing our mind and body for the event. We honour the Goddess, and the celebrants, by dressing up.

Then there is the matter of embarrassment. O.k., we all know that we should not be embarrassed if we meet as nature made us. But most of us even feel embarrassed at being embarrassed. We concentrate so hard on trying to be open-minded and natural that we can't concentrate on the ritual at all. And pretending not to notice someone's sexual response to all those nude dancing bodies, or trying to accept it as 'natural' doesn't make it easier.

Nudity is probably more appropriate to small groups - say, a women-only group celebrating croning, or a couple celebrating their handfasting without witnesses in the woods - than large semi-public events. If you are comfortable celebrating in the nude, and if you are sure all the other participants are as well, don't let me stop you. It's your party.

The other potentially problematic area is physical contact. For many people, hugging each other as part of the ritual is wonderfully soothing, a great affirmation of support. For others it's embarrassing or even scary. Many people are uncomfortable even sitting close to others. I'm one of those people with above-average need for private space. Standing in a crowded underground train with bodies pressed together is my idea of hell. I don't even hug my sisters or close friends, and even touching my lover is something I keep for private moments. No, I don't have hang-ups about my body or theirs. I just value privacy and space, and if someone tries to force me to hug I get stroppy. There are many people like me out there. Equally, there are many who just love the physical affirmation a good hug gives.

If someone doesn't want to hug you, it doesn't mean that they don't like you, that they wish to spoil the ritual, or that you have body odour. Everyone has different needs for physical contact and for private space. Respect this.

On the whole, I've avoided 'hugging sessions' in the rituals in this book. Feel free to add hugs to the ceremony if you wish, particularly on occasions where a hug can give comfort, such as a funeral or a divorce.

Be sensitive to your guests' needs for privacy. If you plan to have all-round hugging at the end of the ritual, suggest that those who don't want it just give a slight shake of their head, so that nobody forces them. If you explain this from the outset, nobody should feel rejected if their offer for a hug is declined.

Invocations

I have not included the casting of a circle as part of the ritual. You can do it if you wish. Personally, I cast a protective circle only if it's a small group. With a large number of people, you face the problem that there may be quite some coming and going. Each time someone needs to fetch a jacket, an asthma inhaler or another candle, or go to the loo, you have to open and close the circle. This disrupts the ritual more than if they just slipped away for a moment. But as I said, it's up to you.

However, I recommend that you do make an invocation. Whether you do it the Wiccan way invoking earth, air, fire, water, Lady and Lord, or any other tradition, it is a good idea to ask for a protective presence. Rituals can be powerful and they affect different people in different ways.

If people of different faiths are present, you may like to encourage them to invoke their own God or Goddess at the beginning of the ritual. Followers of very strict religions -

such as Muslims or Jehova's witnesses - often regard participation in a multi-faith ritual as a great, dangerous adventure. They feel more confident if they can rely on the presence and protection of their God.

It can be a beautiful opening of a ceremony if everyone steps forward to invite their deity or a guardian. But don't force anyone to do this in front of the others if they are shy or just like to keep their religion more private.

Using the poems

Rituals are marvellous opportunities to enjoy poetry. I have included some poems which I find enjoyable on these occasions. If you like them, use them. If not, you may choose others from different sources which move you more. Better still, write your own.

Most of the poems have a rhythmical quality and are meant to be read aloud or chanted. You can even set them to music and sing them if you feel so inclined.

The audience will appreciate the beauty, rhythm, compassion and humour of the poems most if you recite them loudly, slowly and clearly. It helps if you practice this once or twice before the big day.

All the poets in this book will be delighted if you choose to incorporate their poems in your ceremonies. If you need to alter a word or two, to fit your circumstances, please do. The poems are living art, meant to be used and felt and enjoyed, not to be gazed at from a distance.

The poets (Carol Ann Bill, Angela Harrison, Sarah Rooke, Lawrence Long, Linda Vincent), own the copyright to their work, so don't put them on the internet or into your own anthologies without asking first!

Finding a Priestess

For many of the rituals, I have included the role of a 'priestess', in the script. Please don't feel that you have to find a 'real' priestess. A friend or a family member can fulfil this role. Ideally, this should be a mature woman (a crone). Whoever takes on the function, they need to be confident and have a good speaking voice, preferably with experience in leading rituals.

Of course the priestess can be a priest. If you don't like the word priest/priestess, you can refer to them as 'master of ceremonies' or 'mistress of ceremonies', or simply, as 'leader of the ritual'.

If you like to have an ordained priestess or priest, you may find someone within your own religion or spiritual path. If not, just spread the word and ask around. People who may know of someone include teachers of meditation, yoga, shamanism and related subjects, as well as the staff in shops which sell 'new age' type goods. Or contact the Fellowship of Isis, or the Pagan Federation. Both keep registers of ordained priestesses and priests. Their addresses are in the appendix. Enclose a stamped addressed envelope with your query.

Have a chat with your priestess before you invite her, to make sure that your ideas and hers are compatible. You should also discuss whether or not a fee is required. Many priestesses don't have set fees, but accept a gift of money. If she doesn't specify an amount, try to give at least enough to refund her expenses (such as travel, babysitter, incense...).

Chapter 2
Welcoming a Child

This celebration has three functions: to welcome the child, to give the child a name, and to celebrate the mother.

For the child, being born was probably a frightening experience. She'll find the world around her terrifyingly large and cold.

Where does she come from? She doesn't even remember. Where is she going? It will take her days, weeks, years, to find her way and to learn all about her new environment. We want to make her feel welcome, guided and protected.

We also want to give the child a name, or several. A name is something special. Most parents want to give the name formally, with a little ritual, so that the name 'sticks', at least until the child chooses her own name.

Finally, we celebrate the mother and her achievement. In many traditional religions, the mother and her contribution are being ignored. In some patriarchal religions, she is even regarded as 'unclean' for having had sex and carried a child, and rituals are carried out to 'cleanse' her from the original sin. This is hardly an appreciation of nine months pregnancy, labour, and commitment.

Some rituals (especially Pagan rituals) go to the other extreme: The mother is being hailed for having chosen pregnancy (which may or may not have been a matter of intent and choice!). She is also celebrated for dedicating the rest of her life exclusively to the happiness of her child. Again, she may, or she may not. But by assuming, in the wording of the ritual, that she is going to give up her whole self and plan everything around the child, you may induce a feeling of guilt and embarrassment. Especially if she wants to continue her career, and leave the child in the care of a willing grandmother or of foster parents.

In this ritual, we celebrate her for lending her body as a means of transport for the new person.

Choosing Godmothers
For this ritual, you should invite at least three people to be godmothers (or godfathers) to the child.

The responsibilities of the godparents are:

  * To care for the child

  * To protect the child from harm and danger

  * To guide the child during her first years in this world

  * To be points of contact, ports of call when she needs help

  * To assist the parents when they can't cope alone with the task of bringing up the child, for whatever reason

  * If the child loses her parents, to step in and bring her up.

Choose the godparents carefully. Between them, they should be able to fulfill all these functions. Of course, not everyone will be equally good at each task.

Try to get a mix of people for example, someone who can look after the child materially, and someone who can give spiritual riches; someone from within the family and someone from outside; men and women; people belonging to different religions.

If there are people who have already committed themselves to help with the upbringing of the child, then they are the ideal choice. For example, the foster mother, or the father (the one who is the physical father, or the mother's partner who is willing to take on some responsibility). If someone else has the main task of bringing up the child, they too should be involved.

In the case of smaller problems, the godparents will get together and sort out arrangements between them. This is why the godparents should be on friendly terms with each other. It is not a good idea to choose people who are not on speaking terms.

Godparents will also watch over the child's needs which parents may not notice because they are too close. Perhaps parents have not noticed the need for discipline, or for spiritual nourishment, or for more exercise in the fresh air.

Keep written records of the ceremony and who the godparents are. You may like to design a document, and ask the parents, priestess, and godparents to sign this. Make sure all the godparents as well as well as the child herself have a copy.

This can be important if you know there's someone who is just waiting to get their hands on your child if you die. There may be someone who you know will be bad for your child, someone who will shape her exactly the way you didn't want her to be shaped, someone who will use her to take revenge on you. This could be her physical father, or it could be your parents.

Although choosing someone as a godmother doesn't automatically make her the legal guardian if the parents die, a written certificate, signed by witnesses, is a clear record of the parents intent and wishes. It also proves that the godparents were willing, from the start, to take on the responsibility should the need arise.

Why do I emphasise this point? Because I am godmother to one child whom the parents are desperate to save from the clutches of it's grandparents. The parents chose three godparents. All three of us promised that either of us would be willing to bring up the child, and that the other two will support her against any claims the grandparents will make.

It was a Protestant Christian baptism and we made sure the priest knew of the intention and approved of it. There was a bit of a quibble, because the German Protestant rite allowed for two godparents, and also because we godparents were not Protestant Christians. Even the father wasn't, but the parents had decided that the child should be brought up in the mother's faith. After testing us and our intentions thoroughly, the priest agreed to perform the rite.It was a friendly ceremony as part of a church service, with the whole Protestant congregation present as witnesses.

I'm not keen to give up my career and lifestyle to raise someone else's child. But I made the promise that I will, if the need arises.

When to Celebrate

According to a Middle Eastern tradition, the time for a celebration is forty days after the birth. By this time, the mother has probably recovered and is strong enough to participate actively.If the mother wishes, she can organise it herself, or ask the godparents to do the organising.The ritual can be conducted by a priestess, or by a crone.

You need:

* A beautiful throne for the mother. A simple chair or armchair will do, if you drape it with sumptuous fabrics. Some curtains from charity shops with their rich patterns can look royal.

* Flowers. Especially wreaths, necklaces. Also flower petals.
Avoid strong smelling ones.

* Bells. Tiny bells, which you can get from haberdashery shops or pet shops. You can sew them onto ribbons to create musical instruments.

* Candles. White is the traditional colour for new beginnings. You may like to have pink candles for a girl and pale blue for a boy, but you may prefer a light green for new life.

* An image of the Goddess as a mother. E.g. Mary, Isis.

* A certificate (designed by a friend), maybe with several colour photocopies already prepared.

* No incense - at least, no joss sticks or charcoal incense burners. This could be unpleasant for the child. If you feel you need to have a fragrance, use an aromatherapy burner and a few drops of lavender oil. This is light and not smoky.

* Gifts for the child, and a basket to put them in. These can be practical items, such as toys and baby clothes, or symbolic or ritual items. You could make a holly infusion. Break up holly leaves, put them into a saucepan with water, bring to the boil, turn the heat off, let the leaves brew for a few minutes. Then strain and

let it cool. This infusion, sprinkled over a baby at bed time, is believed to protect her from evil influences. Not to be taken internally.

Body of the Ritual

You may need to be a little bit flexible about the ritual. If the child absolutely hates something and starts crying, you may want to shorten it or leave out certain bits. A little bit of crying is no problem, but if the cries are expressions of fear, shorten the ritual.

I recommend that you ask the priestess to cast a protective circle and to invite protective spirits. Alternatively, begin the ritual with a creative visualisation. Imagine the room being filled with a warm pink light.

Place the throne in the centre of the room.

Everyone walks or dances three times clockwise around the room, ringing little bells.

Priestess: '*We have assembled to welcome a child into this world, to bestow a name on her, and to honour the child's mother.*'

Ring bells.

Priestess (leads mother to the throne). '[name], Y*our body is blessed. Thank you for your willingness to carry this child all the way from the Other world to the Earthplane. You have helped to give life. We see the Goddess in you. You are the queen, you deserve the throne. You will experience joy and sorrow from this child. May the experiences always give you strength.*'

Everyone steps forward, draping the mother in flowers or sprinkling rose petals over her, saying a wish for her. For example, *'May you sleep well tonight. Blessed be'*, or *'May you always be well. Blessed be.'*

Now the men stand behind the throne, the women in front of it.

Ring the bells.

Priestess (places the child in the mother's arms):

'Welcome to earth, child. An exciting time awaits you. We introduce you to the earth. Feel it's soil which will give you nourishment.'

She rubs a bit of soil or sand on the child's palms. The child will probably clasp her fist around the finger.

'Feel the air that will carry your speech and thoughts.' For this, the priestess fans the face with a flower.

'See the light that will guide you, the fire that will warm you.'

The priestess holds a candle near the child - very carefully of course.‘

'Feel the water that will keep you clean and refresh you.' For this the priestess warms a few drops of water in her hands, then puts them on the child's forehead.

Ring the bells.

'I name you.....' Now the priestess gives the name or names which the mother or the parents have chosen. If desired, an explanation can be added, e.g. *'I name you Elizabeth in memory of your great grandmother'*.

The priestess takes the child and holds her up.

'Goddess, bless this child. Guide her and protect her. This is ..... [name], may the Goddess always protect her with love.'

The priestess returns the baby to the mother's arms.

Now one after the other of the godparents step forward. Each says:

'I am ... [own name], and I promise today that I will care for this child [child's name], that I will give her guidance, help and protection, as much as I will be able to give when the need arises.' Each godparent signs the document.

Ring the bells.

Then each godparent steps forward and gives a gift in the form of a blessing, combined with a practical item. For example, she may say *'I give you wisdom and understanding'*, and places an illustrated children's encyclopedia in the basket, or *'Skills at arts and crafts'* and crayons. The other guests then give their gifts, such as flowers, toys, baby clothes, also placing them in the basket.

The last godmother, traditionally the oldest, concludes *'And I give you the gift of death, when your time comes, to conclude your life on this earth, because without death there would be no life. May your life on this earth be a fulfilling one.'* Her gift is probably ivy or evergreen.

Everyone: *'So mote it be.'*

Ring the bells.

The priestess (or someone else who is good at singing and chanting) chants the chorus of this poem. The singing should be a happy, rhythmical. Everyone repeats it after her. You can all clap rhythmically if you like. Then she chants or recites the verses, and after each verse everyone joins her in chanting the chorus.

Bírth Chant
by Lawrence Long)
Priestess:
>*'May this child choose peace*
>*May this child choose peace*
>*May this child choose peace*
>*May this child choose peace'*

Priestess:
>*'May this child walk in the green groves of love*
>*May this child love the holy dove'*

Everyone:
>*'May this child choose peace*
>*May this child choose peace*
>*May this child choose peace*
>*May this child choose peace'*

Priestess:
>*'May this child walk in shining days*
>*And use words and music for praise'*

Everyone:
>*'May this child choose peace*
>*May this child choose peace*
>*May this child choose peace*
>*May this child choose peace'*

Priestess:
>*'May this child prosper grow and thrive*
>*Enjoy the blessing of being alive'*

Everyone:

> *'May this child choose peace*
> *May this child choose peace*
> *May this child choose peace*
> *May this child choose peace'*

Priestess:

> *'May this child confer on each she knows*
> *Joy and beauty like the rose'*

Everyone:

> *'May this child choose peace*
> *May this child choose peace*
> *May this child choose peace*
> *May this child choose peace'*

(Everyone chants the chorus)

If you like, you can sing another song, then close the circle. Now that the formal part is over, you may like to put the child to bed, and have a light meal. You can sing, give advice on childcare, recite poetry, whatever. Here's one light-hearted poem which may be suitable for the father to recite:

Someone's Birthday
(by Linda Vincent)
Everyone heard her yell, as it echoed down the hall.
'The baby will be here soon' she heard the midwife call.
Her husband just walked up and down
not knowing what to do.
He held her hand.
She squeezed his tight.
He winced a second or two.

She yelled again.
It made him jump.
His nerves were getting frayed.

She was glad that he was with her.
He wished he hadn't stayed.
Another groan, and baby's head started to appear.
The father's looking queasy now.
'Alright,' he said. '... I'm here'.

Then, the baby shot out like a bullet from a gun,
The doctor caught it in mid-air
like a full-back on the run.
When this pink creation was laid upon her breast,
She smiled at her husband.
He really did his best.
He hadn't ended up lying on the floor.
He was sitting in stunned silence, totally in awe.
He came and kissed her softly.
He was proud; though a little afraid.
He stroked his baby's head.
He was glad that he had stayed.

Chapter 3
Growing Up

When To Celebrate It

Many cultures have a 'growing up' ritual, to celebrate the step from childhood to adulthood. Traditionally, this brought with it the responsibilities of being a woman or being a man.

For example, once you've had your coming of age celebration, you were meant to do a women's (or man's) work. The ritual was usually held when the a young person was judged to be grown up physically, that is, able to father or mother a child. A girl's menarche (first menstruation) and a boy's first 'wet dream' were the visible signs. These were cause for celebration in many societies.

In others, especially patriarchal societies and societies where anything to do with menstruation or sexuality is considered 'unclean', the beginning of the fertile period was something to be ashamed of and hidden, not celebrated. But even these cultures have their coming of age rituals, usually with emphasis on spiritual or moral development.

Growing-up celebrations are sometimes linked to an initiation or spiritual dedication - such as the Christian rite of confirmation, in which the young person consciously, out of her own choice, repeats the pledge her parents made for her when she was a baby.

However, it is a good idea to keep the 'becoming a woman' celebration separate from the spiritual initiation. Both are valuable but involve complex and very different issues. They are worth two celebrations!

Growing-up is in the first place a physical development thing, not a spiritual achievement. It may however mark the beginning of a spiritual quest which lasts for a few months or years, and at the end of which the teenager dedicates herself to her chosen path. I am not giving a ritual for spiritual initiation here, since all religions and traditions have their own very different rites for this, and they don't usually welcome outsiders.

For the 'becoming a woman / becoming a man' party described here, friends and family of any religion and belief can join.

It's not necessary to hold the celebration immediately after the first sign of fertility. Girls may find it a bit embarrassing - and boys almost certainly will. Also, these physical signs often occur at a very early age. A girl who happens to menstruate for the first time at ten years old might find it difficult to appreciate being a woman.

The fourteenth birthday is a good choice - young people are usually ready to assume responsibility and they understand what is behind the ritual. At this age, they also crave excitement and love doing something unusual.

It is up to the parents to decide when their daughter or son is ready. In many ways, the question is not 'Is the teenager ready, mature and responsible enough?' but 'are the parents ready to trust, to encourage and to release their protectiveness?' Traditionally, growing-up rites were often held for groups of youths together, as a tribal festival, so they could not be held in the precise month anyway. You may like to follow this custom and have a joint celebration with others, but most teenagers like to have their own.

Traditions

In the case of growing-up rituals, you will not find much practical inspiration in old customs. If you study books like *The Golden Bough* and *The Mystic Rose* you will be horrified by some of the traditions practiced all over the world

Many existing traditions for the coming of age ceremonies are not at all nice! These often include physical manipulation and mutilation of the body. Ritual circumcision for boys often takes place, which is simply the removal of the foreskin for hygienic and religious reasons.

Among many ethnic groups it has been the custom to rupture a girl's hymen. This was usually done by a crone. But there is also the female circumcision which is still widespread - an operation to remove female genitalia in part or completely. This is sometimes done without an anaesthetic to give the girl the opportunity to prove her ability to withstand pain! This is a cruel mutilation which often cripples a woman mentally and physically.

Once widespread across the world but now less popular, is the following custom, which can be unpleasant and dangerous if carried out strictly. As soon as their puberty starts, girls hide away. They are not to see (or be seen by) men or the sun for several days, months or even years! Interestingly, this particular custom refers to girls only.

Prolonged separation would probably interfere with your daughter's health, social life and education, but if your daughter wants to, she can undergo a day's seclusion in the dark, all on her own or with just her girl friends. This can be a an interesting experience, with mood swings between bored, scared and exhilarated. Afterwards, she is shown to the sun as if she was re-born.

There are quite a few unpleasant customs reserved for boys. A painful tradition you will probably not want to include is to have a tooth knocked out. A boy's initiation into manhood could also involve pulling the beard out, letting it grow to two inches and pulling it out twice more. Not painful, but probably unwelcome nevertheless is the idea to pour melted pig's fat over the body and rub it in to ensure physical strength.

If a boy wants to prove that he can bear pain, you can let him 'run the gauntlet' between other boys - but this should be entirely voluntary and the rules must be laid out clearly to prevent harm and injury.

Whom To Invite

This is definitely a celebration in which the genders are separated. At a ritual for a girl, there should be only women present; at a boy's ritual, only men.

Why? Because a mixed gender event would not have the same atmosphere of trust, relaxation and shared confidences. Allow a teenage girl to choose her guests, and she will inevitably invite the boy on whom she has a wild crush. Instead of being herself, she'll try to impress him. The success of the ritual for her will depend on whether or not she succeeded in making him fall in love with her. Equally, boys that age often feel more like 'real men' if girls are excluded - let them have this pleasure, on this occasion.

The girl's mother or other near female relative is the hostess, with a specially chosen godmother (you may prefer to call her Goddess mother) as the guest of honour. For a boy, the father is the host and a 'godfather' the guest of honour.

All guests should be 'grown women' (or men), that is, older than the celebrant, even if only by a few days. Anyone younger than the celebrant cannot participate. This is symbolic,because the girl leaves her childhood behind and becomes accepted by the adults. It makes the event more 'adult' and exciting.

The teenager chooses whom to invite. The guests can include relatives or friends, or both. A word of warning: relatives and friends often don't mix well! It may be a good idea to choose relatives OR friends.

Let your daughter design and produce the invitation cards, but it is you (for the last time) who issues the invitation.

The Godmother
Invite someone to act as godmother to your daughter. She will be your daughter's sponsor at the ceremony, and act as her guide through adolescent years. The godmother is someone whom you and your daughter trust, someone to whom your daughter can turn when she has a problem - especially when she has a problem with YOU!

So whom do you choose? She should be a mature person, someone who has reached the 'mother phase' or 'crone phase' of her life, someone who has 'seen it all' and can remain calm, a good listener who can keep confidences. An ability to understand teenagers is a great asset. The girl's grandmother or aunt is often a good choice.It is important that the godmother is available and accessible not only during the ceremony, but for the several years to come, so that your daughter can turn to her when she needs help.

If the ceremony is for a teenage boy, you choose a godfather instead.

What You Need For The Ritual

* Decorations (old curtains, fabrics, papier mache, batik-dyed fabrics)

* Candles in colour chosen by teenagers

* Henna (powder, tools, templates, towels, mitts)

* Food (chosen by teenager, suitable for easy preparation -vegetarian burgers are a popular choice)

* A lot of drink (non-alcoholic or alcoholic)

* Drums

* CD or Cassette player

Preparation

Involve your daughter in the preparations as much as possible. Let her choose the music (but encourage her to find something that will appeal to an audience of over 16s), the poem she wants to recite, the guest list, the food, the decorations.

Warning: She may have grand ideas about decorations, a designer gown she absolutely must have, real champagne and lovely presents. But this is a rite which should cost little or nothing.

There's only one way to ensure this: make your daughter pay for everything herself. She'll suddenly become remarkably creative, turning scraps of cardboard into decorations, discovering a fabulous gown at a jumble sale, and inventing a new cocktail based on supermarket lemonade.

Let her choose the 'special colour' for the event. This will be the colour of decorations, altar cloth, candles and so on.

Teenagers have the tendency to choose black. Don't be surprised if your daughter finds it cool to have black candles, a black dress, black fabrics draped everywhere. The effect would be rather gloomy. In addition, black is not a 'power' colour in magic. It has no strength of it's own, and is more suitable for absorbing and neutralizing influences than for giving strength. If she chooses black, ask her to select a secondary colour, to brighten things up and to create a more active magical atmosphere. White (for the maiden) and red (for menstruation) are traditional, but she may have other preferences.

Teenagers may want to smoke cannabis or consume other drugs on this occasion. It is important that your daughter understands that drugs can dull the level of consciousness and devalue the experience. This celebration is about responsibility and awareness, not about escaping into a hazy dream.

To stop other teenagers from supplying drugs at the event, suggest that your daughter writes something along the lines of 'no drugs please' on the invitation. This request should come from the teenager, since such a request from the parent would be ignored. Discuss with your daughter if she wants to include or ban smoking and alcohol.

Set the date several months in advance. This will give you and your daughter the time to produce wonderful decorations, and allows her to plan and carry out her 'challenge'. It will also give her something to look forward to.

If you like, you can swear everyone to secrecy about what's going on at the celebration. This is not strictly speaking necessary - but teenagers like to cloak the ritual in mystery.

Sample Invitation

My daughter Cat (Catherine Yolande Smith) and I are celebrating her 'Becoming a Woman' rite on the occasion of her fifteenth birthday.

We hope you will be able to join us on 16th July from 4 to 8pm in the cellar of our home at 12 The Path, Little Oakhampton.

There will be plenty of vegetarian food, fruit juice and wine.Cat has declared the cellar a 'non-smoking men-free zone', so please leave your cigarettes and boyfriends at home.

No presents please! But if you like, bring a piece of 'wisdom & practical advice' for Cat. She's particularly interested in anything to do with herbs, home-made cosmetics, ancient Egypt and cats, and she plans to collect your ideas and tips in an album.

If you like, dress up in Cat's favourite colours, black and blue - there's a prize for the most imaginative black & blue costume! Bring your drum if you have one, as well as a cassette with your favourite dance music.

Please confirm that you will be coming.

Elizabeth Mountainbrook Smith.

The Challenge

A challenge is an absolute must! Let the teenager set her own challenge. This is usually something which tests her courage, stamina, endurance, creativity, or skill - or a combination of these. The test should be something which stretches the teenagers abilities to the limit, something for which they need preparation and practice.

Here are some ideas for challenges which involve stamina: Swimming across a lake; walking 20 miles around a lake; non-stop dance for several hours (Apache girls do this)

A challenge which tests courage could be spending a night alone in a forest or in a ruined castle. On the other hand, it could be something which involves the courage to face a personal phobia. Someone with a fear of heights could climb a high tower; someone with a phobia of fire could go on a fire fighting course; someone who is scared of snakes could allow a python being draped around her neck and someone who gets sick at the sight of needles and syringes could donate blood.

Alternatively, she could set herself a skills test. The traditional embroidery samples for example measured a girl's needlework skills; when the sampler was complete, she was considered grown up. Your daughter could create wood-carved table or write a volume of poetry in beautiful calligraphy and bind the book herself.

Just make it very clear that you are not going to finance costly adventures. Yes, it would be exiting to go deep-sea diving in the Red Sea, but your daughter must seek her adventure closer to home.

While the teenager suggests her own challenge, it is for the godmother to decide if it is acceptable. The godmother may insist on making it more difficult. On the other hand, she may stop your daughter from a night hike with her friends in an area where a serial killer operates. As a parent, you have to trust your daughter and her godmother to choose a challenge responsibly and to take all necessary precautions for health and safety. Your daughter is growing up now - this is your opportunity to learn not to worry about her!

Gifts

Every guest also brings a piece of wisdom or advice, for example, a cooking recipe, tips for contraception, hairstyling advice. If they like, they can write it down. Those who can't or don't want to write, can produce a drawing instead.The girl gives her godmother a present, something which has personal meaning but does not cost anything.

The only present of any serious monetary value which may be given is from the mother to the godmother, in appreciation of the help she has pledged for the coming years. There is an Apache custom that the parents of the growing-up girl give the godmother stacks of food preserves, clothes, even a horse. You don't have to be quite so practical. An item of jewellery may be more personal.

The mother gives the daughter a 'moon' necklace - see below. Both the mother and the godmother can give the girl her first ritual tools. These need not be a complete set (bear in mind that this is not a spiritual initiation), and should not be expensive, but lovingly chosen. Since mother, godmother and daughter may belong to different spiritual traditions, the presents may represent different religions. For example, a pretty chalice from a car boot sale, a koran, a bible, a prayer-book, a book of spells, a herbal, a staff, a goddess statue, a rosary. Alternatively, mother or godmother can give her a book on sexuality, which will help her understand what is going on with her body.

The Moon Necklace

This gift from the mother to her daughter refers to the girl's 'moon flower', (the monthly period) and her membership of the 'moon-lodge' (the community of women). The necklace can be self-made or purchased, but it should not be of great monetary value. Here are some ideas.

If your daughter is interested in ethnic jewellery, then the filigree crescent moon necklaces of Southern Egypt, the crescent moon necklaces of the Malays or an Indian sandalwood necklace will appeal.

If you are artistic, you can make a crescent-moon shaped pendant from any material.

Less spectacular-looking but easy to make is a tiny herb sachet. Use a small piece of cotton, heap dried 'moon plants' onto it such as lemon rind, gardenia, Irish moss, grape seeds, bladderwrack, mallow, willow leaves and lemon balm, tie it with a string, ready.

If you don't have the imagination, time or talent to make your daughter's moon necklace, you can go to a jeweller's and buy a small silver moon-shaped pendant. Or go to one of the many occult/magic/crystal shops and buy a small stone pendant. Moonstone, aquamarine, quartz or chalcedony are suitable.

A father's traditional gift to a boy is a hunting weapon. Today, this can be a practical tool such as a Swiss army knife. It could also be a decorative ethnic weapon such as a boomerang or a carved spear, or perhaps quiver of self-made arrows.

Body of the Ritual
The mother explains why everyone has assembled here.

Play drums to raise power.

The teenager talks about her 'challenge', what she did, why she chose this, how it worked out.

The teenager presents a song or poem of her choice which has meaning for her on this occasion. Here are two suggestion:

Time of Tides
(by Lawrence Long)

I am come into the time of blood
The time of tides
I am come into the time of good
Between my sides

I am come into the time of fruit
Upon the bough
I am come into the time of pursuit
And love to show

I am come into the time of child
A time of pain
I am woman strong and mild
Strong in the rain

I am come into the time of blood
The time of tides
I am come into the time of good
Between my sides

The Mother's Clan
(by Kazz)

Re-attuning to Goddess Moon
Divine feminine waxes lyrically
As Maidens and Mothers bloom.

Ebbing and flowing
Awareness is growing
And we Her children
Gain insight and knowing.

Of that which we realised
Within for so long
Harmonising with Mother Nature
Spinning Her labyrinth song

Upon the Sacred path
Dancing in love and light,
Re-uniting our Mother's clan
Integrating, blessings, oh so bright.

I have tried to find a suitable poem for a boy, and even encouraged poets to write one. But the results were all either too wise and subtle to be appreciated by a boy of that age, or too explicit and rude! So you'll have to write your own poem. If you are pleased with it, send to me c/o the publishers, and who knows, we may ask your permission to include it in future editions...

The teenager lights the candles.

The godmother explains the 'facts of life': menstruation, sexuality, conception, pregnancy, contraception, phases of life, all in a positive way. To make the girl feel less embarrassed, the godmother can deal with it in a 'of course you know all this so let's just recap it for ritual's sake' manner. But never take it for granted that teenagers really know everything. It is surprising what dangerous gaps there are in their knowledge.

If the godmother is too embarrassed to talk about these matters, she can present the teenager with an informative book about the subject, and make the handing over of the book special.

During this talk, you may like to follow the old Arabic custom, of having the girl's hands henna'd for the first time. The henna artist creates the red patterns on the back of the girl's hands, and tints her finger tips orange. I'm not talking about fake 'henna tattoos' but about the real thing, the mixing of the greenish henna powder with water, the careful application of it through cut-out paper templates. This is a traditional feminine activity to mark special occasions. It is exciting and soothing. There's something going on to watch, so the talk is less likely to be embarrassing.

During this, there will also be time for the girl to ask questions. Anything that bothers or worries her, or that she is curious about. The older woman answers all her questions frankly.

Applying henna needs skill, patience and a steady hand. The patterns remain visible for several days, then fade gradually. Whoever is applying it should try it out on herself or another friend before the ceremony, using the same brand and the same instructions, to avoid accidents and disappointments. In the Middle East, the women call in a professional henna artist for the occasion. Check how long the henna needs to dry. If the girl has to keep her hands in mitts for five hours, you may have to alter the order of the ritual or choose a different henna preparation.

The mother gives the girl her moon necklace, and blesses her. (The father gives the son a 'hunting weapon' and blesses him).

The teenager pours a drink for everyone.

Everyone presents their 'piece of advice' and their present.

The teenager serves the food or opens the buffet, and turns on the music. If she likes, she can perform a solo dance with her favourite music, but this is optional.

Time for informal partying and dancing.

Chapter 4
Handfasting (Wedding)

All religions and legal systems have their own standardised rites to mark the beginning of a marriage. Yet there are many couples who are looking for something a bit 'different', for a variety of reasons.

You may find that the brief event at the registrar's office isn't personal or joyful enough. Or you may have chosen a big church wedding and reception 'for the family', and want an additional, more intimate, celebration just for yourself and a few chosen friends.

Perhaps there's something about your relationship that isn't accepted for conventional ceremonies. For example, one of you may be divorced and not be free to re-marry in the eyes of your church, or perhaps you and your partner belong to the same gender and the law in your country doesn't recognise your partnership.

One couple for whom I organised a handfasting lived in America and wanted to fulfill their dream of getting married in England. The British registrar's offices would have required a long period of stay in the UK before the ceremony, which would have made it too expensive. Other couples wished to get married in Arabic costume, or on the beach, or in a boat on the river.

All these requests can be fulfilled if you do your own ritual, perhaps after you've been to the registrar's for the legal bit.

The beginning of marriage is a joyous occasion, whether you call it 'handfasting', 'tying the knot', 'jumping over the broom' or 'wedding'. There's something special about a wedding; everyone likes to celebrate it. People may hesitate about accepting an invitation to a name-giving, a croning, or a death celebration. But they can't resist a wedding.

Whenever I organise an 'alternative wedding ceremony' for someone, people around me drop hints that they would like to participate, even if they don't know the couple. You, too, may find that many people would like an invitation.

Perhaps this is why in many countries the celebrations are spread out over several days. You have a day for the women, a day for the men, a day for the relatives, a day for the friends, and so on. Spreading the events over several days allows for more leisure and relaxation, and makes them less hurried and stressful for the couple. Of course, the couples leave all the organising to their families.

Customs and Traditions

There are so many wedding traditions that you are spoilt for choice. I have selected favourite elements which are common in many cultures. If you like traditions, you can add them to my rituals. They will be extra adornments. If possible, choose customs from your own, and your partner's, ethnic backgrounds and religions, as well as from the old traditions of the country in which you are living, plus anything that is meaningful to you.

Have a look in books about wedding customs, or in books like 'The Golden Bough' or 'The Mystic Rose'. You'll find rituals which are amusing and entertaining, but also some which are hair-raising, scary, cruel and suited to put anyone off the idea of marriage. Here are some suggestions which are user-friendly:

Abducting the bride

Where I come from in southwest Germany, the bride's friends (male and female) abduct her during the reception and take her to a secret place. This is usually a pub of her choice. The bride of course is very willing and offers only token resistance. To make the abduction more difficult, there is a rule that the bride's bouquet has to go with her. It's the chief bridesmaid's task to guard the bouquet during the reception, in order to prevent the abduction. The kidnappers employ all kinds of tricks to distract her from her task.

The groom and his male friends, once they've discovered the bride's disappearance, have to find her. I remember one wedding where I helped to kidnap the bride. We got a particularly handsome young man to charm the chief brides- maid while I snatched the bouquet and threw it out of the window for the others to catch. The bride desired champagne in the bar of the town's most exclusive restaurant. We were found out quickly. 'Easy,' said the groom. 'I know her taste for expensive drinks.'

The groom pays the bill for everyone. Then he takes his bride back to the reception, where they are greeted with cheers. Only then are they allowed to depart for their wedding night and honeymoon.

Belly dancing

In many countries in North Africa and the Middle East, a wedding is not complete without a belly dancer. This is an ancient tradition, going back much further than Islam. It probably stems from thousands of years ago, when dancing was used in worship of a great Mother Goddess. The movements were used to bring the blessing of fertility to the couple.

Later, when women and men led separate lives and the couple might not have seen each other before the wedding, the belly dancer's function was to put them in them in the mood for the wedding night. This is often misconstrued as sexual titillation aimed at the groom. But more importantly, the dance serves to put the virgin bride at ease about her body and about her role as a woman. A good belly dancer who understands the tradition, aims her dance more at the bride than at the groom. She is called 'sheikha' (the woman who knows), 'almeh' or 'alima' (both meaning 'educated entertainer').

In Morocco, there is the tradition of the 'shikkatt'. This is a pre-wedding dance. While the women and the men celebrate the forthcoming event in separate tents, the sheikha visits first the women. She demonstrates dance movements which are copied by the other women. These are often quite explicit, explaining the facts of life from sexual coupling to childbirth. Everyone enjoys this hilarious entertainment, including the bride. Having spent all her life among nomads and working with goats, camels and other animals, she is probably familiar with mating and birth, and can enjoy the display.

Afterwards, the sheikha goes to the men's tents where she repeats her dance... just in case the groom doesn't know what is expected of him that night.

There may also be a special bridal procession called 'zeffat al aroussa', where everyone joins in the dancing.

If you want to get a belly dancer for a wedding, try to find one knows about the old customs. Youth and prettiness are not important on this occasions. You want a woman with experience, who is a great entertainer and who understands her ancient role.

I work as a professional belly dancer (under my stage name, 'Almeh Amira' - you may have seen me on the telly), and I love performing at weddings. Interestingly, it is almost always the bride who chooses to have a belly dancer at her wedding.

First I perform solo dances, then I hand out drums, tambourines and finger cymbals and lead everyone in the zeffat al aroussa. I seat the bride and the groom in the centre of the dance floor and I present a comedy act in which I have some saucy fun with the two - but nothing explicit or embarrassing. Finally, I give a present to the bride.

Everyone loves it. Children are always the first to join in. A belly dancer adds colour and excitement to the reception, and looks good in the photo album and on the video. If you have difficulty locating a good belly dancer in your area, write to me (c/o the publishers) enclosing 2 first class stamps, and I'll help you find one.

Bath day and henna night

Surprisingly many traditions include a ritual bath a day or two before the wedding. No doubt the origins of this custom lie in sensible hygiene, especially in places where water is scarce and daily bathing not possible. You want your partner to be clean for the wedding night.

But the bride's bath is not just an ordinary bath, it's a ceremony in itself. Her girlfriends prepare the bath, making the water fragrant with rose petals, dry her with soft towels, massage the the skin of her body with flower oils, and care for her hair. The bride will be pampered so that she feels relaxed about her body and beautiful.

Perhaps you and your friends could enjoy a day out at your nearest hammam (steam bath), as the brides in Turkey, the Middle East and North Africa do? This can be wonderfully relaxing, social experience, which will leave you feeling refreshed and squeaky clean.

In the Middle East and North Africa, there is also the custom of 'henna night', another girls-only event. The bride has her hands painted in elaborate henna patterns. These are usually dark red geometrical patterns, with the finger tips died orange. The hair may also be given a henna treatment for a red shine, and additional patterns may be painted on the face. Of course I'm talking about real henna, not about the so called 'henna tattoos' which have little in common with the real thing. Preparing real henna paste is a ritual. One of the few acceptable careers for a woman in traditional areas in the Middle East and North Africa is that of a self-employed henna artist. There are now professional henna-artists in the west, too, but a patient friend with a steady hand can do it for you.

Read the instructions. Henna takes a long time to set, during which you may need to wear mittens.

Depending on the type of henna used, the method of applying, and the natural condition of your skin, the henna patterns will stay on for three to nine days. Brides in Tunisia especially love henna night. An ancient custom decrees that the new bride does not need to do any housework until all the henna patterns have worn off.

The Meaning of Marriage

In most countries in the western world, marriage is between two people of different gender. It begins with the wedding and ends with the death of one of the partners.There may, or may not, be an 'escape clause' allowing a divorce if the marriage does not work.

In other cultures and traditions, there are variations. For example, in some Middle Eastern and African societies, a man may have more than one wife. In some societies in the past, a woman could have more than one husband. Some societies accept marriages between homosexual couples.

Marriage was often for a specific time only, for example in some North American and some Chinese ethnic groups there were customs that marriage was only for four years, or until the first child was born, and could be renewed if both partners wished.

Some Pagan groups maintain that marriage is for 'a year and a day' only, or for 'nine years'. Others say that marriage is not just for one life, but for eternity.

Give some thought to this. For how long do you wish your marriage to last? You can choose any period that suits you. You don't even have to tell your family and wedding guests that you have committed yourselves to nine years only. But it is important that you both know and agree what you are letting yourselves in for. If one of you assumes that you are celebrating a 'year and a day' wedding, while the other believes herself married for life, this can have tragic consequences.

While you are in love, you may wish your love and your marriage to last forever, but is this realistic? You are both going to change during your life, and the world in which your marriage is situated is going to change as well. About one in three conventional marriages ends in divorce; and many marriages are dead inside and retain only a facade for the outside world.

Are you contemplating a commitment for all future lives? How well do you know your partner? Have you thought about the opposition your commitment may meet in another life, when you may belong to different tribes at war with each other, or families where the parents arrange marriages? Can you know how your partner's personality will develop in a different historical period, in a different society? You may not even like him.

Many couples choose the safe option. They get married for a year and a day, which is perhaps the equivalent of conventional engagement, or a modern marriage on trial. If they are still happy after the year, they marry for nine years (or whatever seems sensible). After that, they can renew this commitment or make a vow for a lifetime. Only towards the end of their lives, they consider a commitment for eternity.

The Priestess

Whether it's for a specific period or forever, marriage is a serious commitment. This is reflected by having a priestess prepare the couple and conduct the ceremony. To find an ordained priestess who can conduct the ritual, ask around. Members of the Fellowship of Isis or of the Pagan Federation can often help.

If you cannot find an ordained priestess willing to carry out the ritual you have chosen, you can ask a crone to take on the role.

Pre-Wedding Talks

The priestess will probably insist on meeting you before she agrees to marry you. She will test your sincerity and ask you a lot of questions about the chosen ritual, about you, your partner, and your attitudes and expectations of marriage.

Very often, she will require more than one meeting. She may want to meet you both together, and also separately. Her questions may be probing and challenging. Sometimes you may find the questions unpleasant or you may get bored and ask why she doesn't just marry you.

But the pre-wedding talk is important. This is to help you spot the problems which might destroy your marriage if you are not careful. When you are in love, your feelings, your desires and your ideals make objective assessment nearly impossible. You will be aware of differences in your lifestyles and expectations, but you are not aware just how critical they can be.

If you are genuinely in love, it's natural to think 'We'll work it out', 'Love conquers all', or 'When the baby is here he'll love it', or 'Once we're married she'll understand that I don't want my wife to go out to work' or 'she'll never find out'.

Most religions have a pre-wedding talks and seminars as a requirement before their priests or priestesses agree to marry the couple. I attended a wedding in Malta, a catholic country. The catholic church does not permit artificial contraception. But before my friends could get married, they attend several weeks of regular evening classes, learning among other things about how to use natural contraception methods.They also learnt about sex, monthly periods, pregnancy and much more, a lot of which was new ground for the young man.

Of course, the pre-wedding talk or talks are particularly important if you and your partner have not known each other for very long, perhaps because it was love at first sight and you decided to get married quickly, or because yours is an arranged marriage.

Questions your priestess may ask you include sensitive subjects such as:

> * Is this going to be a commitment for a lifetime? Or for a shorter period? Why did you choose this particular period? What is your opinion about divorce?

> * Do you expect sexual fidelity from your partner? Are you prepared to be sexually faithful? If you both agree on sexual fidelity, what happens if one of you breaks this promise? Will you tell? Will this end the marriage?

If you allow each other sex with other people, will this be open or discreet? Will you allow only casual encounters, or affairs, or longer-term relationships? Will you bring your sexual partners into your home? How are you going to protect yourselves from sexually transmitted diseases?

* Do you plan to have children? How many? Who is going to care for them? Are you going to use contraceptives? Which methods?

* How important is your religion to you? What does your religion require of you? How much time do you spend in worship? In which religion will you bring up your children? Does your religion make demands or restrictions on your marriage and family life, if so, which? Are there going to be clashes? How will your family and friends react to your partner's religion (e.g. what will they say when they find out you've married a witch?)

* How important is your work and career for you? Do you plan to continue working after the wedding? After the birth of your child? May your career require relocation? Do you expect your family to follow you if you move to another town? Does your career require help from your partner (e.g. hosting dinners for business clients, keeping the books)? Are you prepared to give up your circle of friends, your clubs, hobbies and career to relocate with your partner? Are you willing to support your partner's career?

* How much privacy do you need? How much time do you want to spend with your partner ever week, every day? Which hobbies, club memberships and social obligations do you want to continue after your wedding, after the birth of your child? How much time will take? Do you expect to share a bed with your partner, or do

you want your own bed? Your own bedroom? Your own bathroom?

* Who is contributing what to the housework? How much housework are you willing to do, and what do you expect your partner to do? Do you expect supper on the table when you come home?

* How much do you earn? Do you know what your partner's income is? Are you going to share your income? Are you going to have separate accounts? Will you have a joint household bank account? Who is going to be in charge of the household finances?

* In whose name will the mortgage be? Which items will you own jointly, which will be separate? What will you pay for individually? What happens to the mutual possessions if you split up?

* What are your sexual needs and habits? How often do you expect to have sex with your partner? Do you know how often he expects to have sex with you? Love and consideration can help to bridge gaps, but if one of you wants sex five times daily and one wants it only once a month, your marriage will be tested severely! If you are experienced at practicing sex, you can probably assess not only how much sex you want, but also what exactly you want. What are your sexual preferences and deviations? If you make love only when wearing a rubber suit, you'd better tell your partner now. And what are your partner's kinks? Are they compatible? If not, what are you going to do about it?

Preparation

Whatever format you decide your wedding is going to have, don't organise your own wedding. I repeat: don't organise your own wedding. I have seen too many brides looking stressed and shattered at their own ceremony, unable to enjoy themselves because they were frantically trying to cope with last-minute problems.

It's not just the organising and preparing that's taking the energy out of you. The worst is the trouble-shooting. Things are bound to go wrong. And to whom do people turn when there is trouble during the ceremony? Who has to fix it? The person who set it all up in the first place, of course.

No, my friend. You make a few choices about what your wedding should involve - say, the venue, a few customs, your favourite music, the type of entertainment, the dress. Then you hand over the organising to someone else. This could be your mother or a friend, someone who enjoys organising and who is good at it. Trust them completely. Don't control all their decisions; allow them to surprise you. All you have to do is go to your wedding and enjoy it.

The Night Before

The eve of the wedding day is often the occasion for a big party. In Britain, men and women celebrate separate 'hen nights' and 'stag nights', doing mildly naughty things such as watching a stripper, for the bride and the groom to enjoy one last moment of freedom.

In southwest Germany, we have instead a Polterabend. Yes, it's 'Polter' as in 'Poltergeist', and that's what it is about. We have a party to drive away spirits who might harm the couple. For this, everyone, women, men, children, arrive equipped not only with food and drink to share, but also with baskets of chipped and ugly looking crockery.

When everyone has had some food and drink, we go outside and line up some distance from a wall. We throw the plates against the wall, smashing them with as much noise as possible. The noise will drive the most persistent of ill-wishing spirits away.

The plate smashing is great fun. At least, it's great fun for the guests. Maybe less so for the couple, who have to get a broom, a dustpan, a brush, and a bin, and clear all the crockery shards away.

Many of my friends and neighbours used to hoard odd bits of crockery in anticipation of the next Polterabend. Some people go and buy cheap crockery to smash, which always struck me as sinful waste. If you want to introduce the custom of a Polterabend before your wedding, get your crockery from car boot fairs and boot sales. Plates and saucers are easiest to smash.

Invite all your neighbours to participate in the activity, then they won't mind the noise so much. And finally - try not to celebrate for too long, or with too much alcohol. You'll find it difficult to enjoy your wedding day if you are tired and have a splitting headache. Of course, you could always celebrate your 'night before' a several nights before the event.

You Need:
    * A large room - or hire a hall.

    * Incense. Rose and jasmine are traditional. Candles. White, pink, red and green are traditional colours.

    * Scarves. The bride and the groom need a scarf or handkerchief each, preferably decorated by themselves. If you have nimble fingers and enjoy needlework, you can hem and embroider squares of delicate fabric. A

quicker method is to buy two handkerchiefs and fabric-paint, glitter-paint or glitter-glue (from haberdasheries or fabric shops) in several colours, and apply the paint directly from the bottle. It's quick and it will look spectacular. You can also use textile glue to apply sequins

* Food and drink (especially honeyed sweets and wine)

* Two chairs for the couple.

* A canopy or arch, decorated with flowers (roses if possible).

* Lots of flowers to decorate the room. Seasonal flowers picked from the meadow or the garden are better than hothouse flowers. Red and pink are the best colours. But you may have to compromise. I remember organising a wedding in November when there was not a single bloom in our garden. So I used autumn leaves, rosehips, haws, and just a few purchased hothouse flowers.

* Flowers which bring luck at a wedding are yarrow, hawthorn blossoms, roses, orange blossoms, myrtle and quince blossoms. However, most of them are considered a fertility blessing - maybe that's not what you want from marriage.

* Rice and nuts, if desired

 * Red pink and white ribbons.

* A bouquet for the bride. This should contain myrtle blossom, orange blossom, rose, and yarrow. The yarrow is supposed to guarantee seven years of married bliss, so don't forget it. It flowers in the late summer; dry it for a winter wedding

* Baskets with pink red and white flower petals for bridesmaids.

* Two brooms.

* A marriage certificate. It should contain the names of couple, the date, the names of the priestess and the witnesses, and leave room for the signatures.

* Drums, tambourines, finger cymbals and musical instruments (or cassette/CD player). The couple choose their favourite pieces of music or songs. Look at traditional wedding tunes from many cultures, or historical melodies.

* Little bells.

* Everyone should be dressed up beautifully and imaginatively, preferably with flowers somewhere, e.g. wreaths of flowers on the head.

Decorating the Room

If you have a garden and if the weather is fine, you can celebrate outdoors. You may not need to do much decorating then. Just set up the arch or the canopy, and place the two chairs underneath.

Otherwise, place flowers and ribbons everywhere.

Set up the canopy or arch in the middle of the room, with the two chairs underneath.Light the candles and the incense just before the procession arrives. Make sure they are in safe places where they can't get knocked over or set fire to curtains.

Body of the Ritual
(Big ritual with priestess, witnesses and guests)

Two witnesses with the two brooms, and the musicians with their instruments are already in the hall.

Carry out a procession to the hall where the ceremony will take place. First walks the priestess, then the bridesmaids, then the couple, then the wedding guests. Play drums, finger cymbals, tambourines and other instruments. The bride carries the bouquet, the bridesmaids little flower baskets from which they strew petals. The procession can be quite long if there are many people.

When the procession reaches the door to the hall, the musicians play. The witnesses stand either side of the door. They let the priestess and bridesmaids pass. But they cross the broomstick so that they form a low arch under which the couple has to pass. Then they take the brooms and go to the canopy.

In the meantime, the procession moves three times clockwise around the room, with music, the towards the canopy. The priestess and the bridesmaids stand aside. The witnesses kneel on the floor each holding both brooms in both hands, so that they form a low hurdle. The couple have to jump over the hurdle, then they can take a seat. Everyone cheers, and the bridesmaids throw the last flower petals over the couple. The people who hold bells ring them.

The chorus of the marriage chant is always recited by both partners together, the verses only by one. If you don't enjoy chanting, you can simply recite it

Marriage Chant
(by Lawrence Long)

Couple:
'We are bonding, handfasting, tying the knot
We are sharing what we have got
We have a lot'

Bride:
'We are bringing bodies, we are bringing souls
we are cool as water, we are hot as coals
We are trysting, we are kissing
Like waterfalls

'Couple:
'We are bonding, handfasting, tying the knot
We are sharing what we have got
We have a lot'

Groom:
'We are eating, we are mating
We are turning, relating
We are changing, uniting
We are bringing the night in'

Couple:
'We are bonding, handfasting, tying the knot
We are sharing what we have got
We have a lot'

Bride:
'We are joyous, we are glorious
Love, it is victorious
over hating, over warring
Over everything that's boring'

Couple:
We are bonding, handfasting, tying the knot
We are sharing what we have got
We have a lot'

Groom:
'Bless our union, bless our oneness
Bless our daytime, bless our undress
Bless our holding, bless our moulding
Bless this warmth to put our cold in

Couple:
'We are bonding, handfasting, tying the knot
We are sharing what we have got
We have a lot'

Everyone:
'We are bonding, handfasting, tying the knot
We are sharing what we have got
We have a lot'

Ring the bells.

Now the couple say their own vows, in their own words. This is more natural, more moving, and more sincere than any prescribed formula. For example 'I promise to honour and cherish you for the rest of this our live together, to protect you with all my strength, and to help you raise the children you already have, and the children with which we may be blessed together.' or 'Thank you agreeing to share the rest of this life with me. I promise that I will always be there for you when you need me, to give you companionship and support. I will give you as much freedom as you need, and whenever our work commitments separate us for a time, I will wait for your return.' Promise whatever is meaningful to you, and what you intend to keep.

Ring the bells.

One of the witnesses takes the bride's bouquet from her hands.The second witness gives the priestess the scarves.The priestess ties the scarf decorated by the bride around the right wrist of the groom (around the left wrist if he is left handed), and the groom's scarf around the bride's wrist.

Priestess: *'Is it your wish that I unite you today in marriage?'*

Couple: *'It is.*

'The priestess takes the couples hands and binds them together by knotting the scarves.

Priestess: *'Goddess, bless this couple and their marriage. Bless them with love. Bless them with harmony to enjoy the good days, and with strength to endure the bad days'*

'Everyone: *'Blessed be'*.

'The priestess now unties the couple by removing the knots which tie the scarves to the wrists, but so that the knot holding the scarves together remains. She retains the scarf as a record of the marriage.

Now the couple each present their own contribution to the ceremony. This could be a dance, a poem, a song, or something entirely different. If they are creative people, then it can be a dance they have choreographed, a poem they have written, a song they have composed. They can present a joint contribution, or each presents something separately. The most unusual artistic contribution I've ever seen was at a wedding I organised. The couple performed an improvised sword dance together, each holding a sword and touching each other with it. They managed to make this look fierce and tender at the same time.

For those among you who are less artistically inclined, there are many love poems available in literature that you can recite. Here is a little known one that will appeal to those with an interest in Egyptian traditions:

Egyptian Love Song   (by Sarah Rooke)

My love crossed over the Great River
Only to be by my side
Across from the hungry crocodiles, fear aside
He spears the beast for my sake

The sweet song of the swallow flies on overhead
Above the Pharaoh's Lake, a thousand stars
Oh- when I am in Neterkert, let my soul shine
amongst them together with my love
Let Eternity strive to tear us apart
For I shall be with you forever from the start

Eyes of lapis lazuli, lips full as Pharaoh's wine
Skin as smooth as marble, hair raven black
You light my way with a sign
Your beauty I admire
You give me hope, you renew my desire
Let not the Gods punish me in the fire!
If your soul I should ever impire
Across the desert, I hear your gentle voice call
Lost in the darkness of the tomb
Let me light your way out of the gloom

I hear my love call to me
His voice beckons to me
Across the desert, across the sea
Across the fiery sands, across the cool water
Look, look with your heart, my love
Until it is me you truly find

The couple, the priestess, and both witnesses sign the marriage certificate. If several copies have been prepared, they should sign all the copies. The bride, the groom and the priestess should each have a copy as a record of the event.

The couple sit down again. Everyone dances in a circle, clockwise, around the couple. Choose happy, bouncy music for this, preferably live music. Irish or Scottish folk music, some of the livelier tunes of medieval or Tudor music, a modern love happy love song (*'Congratulations and Jubilations...'*), the Arabic *Zeffat Al Aroussa*, or maybe *Mabrouk Mabrouk* by Noor Shamaal are all suitable. If the wedding is themed, choose something that suits the theme. You can play drums, finger cymbals and ring little bells.

If you like, you can encourage the wedding guests to throw rice over the bridal couple, and the couple reciprocate by throwing nuts (carefully!). Both nuts and rice are meant to bring wealth, fertility and general good luck.

Serve the food and drink, or open the buffet.

Then comes the entertainment, for example: The band can play music for everyone to dance to. Some of the guests may have prepared a speech, a game or a comedy act. Friends may kidnap the bride. The belly dancer comes on and does her bit.

Small Ritual
If you'd like to keep your bonding private, you can carry out a ritual all by yourself, without a priestess, witnesses, guests and entertainment.

This is particularly suitable if you want to commit yourself only for the 'a year and a day' period, or if you want to keep the wedding secret, or if you want to renew the marriage vow when the initial period has expired, or if you have been married to each other for a long time and now want to make the commitment for eternity.

You need a knife, a candle in a protective container, matches, possibly a bowl of water, wine and a drinking vessel, and some sweet food such as a honey cake.

Go to an old tree which stands in a secluded place, preferably near a stream, lake, pond, river or sea.

'We ask the guardian spirit of the earth to be present and to be our witness.'

Bend to touch the ground with your hands, feel the sand or the soil or the grass.

'We ask the guardian spirit of the air to be present and to be our witness.

Hold your hands up, feel the wind or the stillness of the air on your palms.

'We ask the guardian spirit of the fire to be present and to be our witness.'

Light the candle, hold your hands close to it.

'We ask the guardian spirit of the water to be present and to be our witness.'

Go to the pond or the river, dip your hands into it. If there is no water nearby, dip your fingers into the bowl of water.

'Spirit of the tree, we ask you to witness our pledge and to bear our record of it.'

Place the knife underneath the tree.

'Great Goddess, Mother Nature, be with us today as we pledge ourselves in your name.

'Go to the tree, hold your partner's hands so that the tree is between you. Dance three times clockwise around the tree.

First partner: 'Under this tree, today, in the presence of the spirit of the tee and the guardian spirits of the elements and the Great Goddess Nature, I pledge myself in marriage to you for [state intended period].

'The second partner repeats the words.

Now fasten your hands together. For this, you cross your wrists so that your right wrist is over your left wrist. Your right hand holds your partner's left hand, and your left hand hold's your partner's right hand.

Now you say your own vows, in words and contents that are meaningful to you.

Take the knife and carve your initials into the tree's trunk. Do this tenderly. There is no need to make large cuts. It's not necessary for passers-by to see the initials from a distance. Small initials are enough, just big enough for the tree to bear the mark as a record of your pledge. Lovers have carved their initials into trees for centuries.

Pour wine into the drinking vessel. Each holds the cup for the other to drink from. Leave a bit of wine in the cup and pour it out as an offering for the tree.

Take the honey cake, break of a piece and feed it to your partner, who then does the same for you. Leave a few crumbs of the cake under the tree, as an offering for the tree.

'Spirit of the tree, thank you for being witness to our marriage and for carrying the mark of our pledge.Spirits of the earth, of the air, of the fire and of the water, thank you for being present in our ritual. Protect the marriage that you have witnessed.Great Goddess, Mother Nature, bless our marriage with you love. Give us harmony to enjoy the good days, and strength to endure the bad. We are now husband and wife.

So mote it be.'

(Editors note: Those who do not wish to carve the tree might symbolically draw the initials on it weith water or wine)

Chapter 5
Home Blessing

Moving into a new home is a positive step. It is often connected with other significant changes: You may move house because of a new job, because you have got married, because you are expecting a baby. Perhaps you were evicted from your previous home or could not afford the rent or the mortgage anymore, or decided you did not want to share with the same flatmates any longer. You may have separated from a partner, or are leaving the safety and confines of your parents' home for the first time, or perhaps good fortune has brought you a windfall and you can finally move into the spacious and comfortable place you've always dreamt of.

Moving home is a time of excitement and adventure. The home is yours, to decorate, furnish and use as you please. It is your sanctuary, the place where you are safe from most dangers and threats. It is also a time of chaos and anxiety. Packing and unpacking, transport, cleaning, all needs to be done usually within a short time. You may feel pressurised and exhausted.

Finally, it is a time of reassessment of your life, your values, your tastes. When packing, you decide which items from your old life you keep, and which you discard. You decide if you need new, different colours in your life, and discard your old colour schemes. It's a kind of inner renewal and purification process.

Moving home definitely calls for a ritual!

Whom to Invite

You can invite whoever you like, as long as you are certain that they genuinely wish you well. You don't want anyone who holds a grudge against you to step over your threshold.

Children, adults, colleagues, friends, club members, family members, new neighbours are all welcome.

It is a good idea to have a priestess conduct the ritual. But if you prefer, you can ask a friend to act as mistress of ceremonies and carry out the role I've allocated to the priestess.

Preparing the Ritual

Don't think for a moment that your home has to be completely decorated, furnished and tidied up before the ritual. If you wait until everything is just perfect, you'll never get round to doing the ritual. Do it as soon as possible, preferably on the day before you spend the first night in the house.

If many of your belongings are still in cardboard boxes, just pile the boxes into the centres of the rooms (not along the walls), so that the procession can move around them. Try to keep one room, or one area of a room, free from clutter. Lay out rugs and cushions.

Try out your fireplace or heater to make sure it's in good working order. Make sure that the immediate needs of party guests can be met - these include toilet paper, corkscrew and bottle opener, a cassette player and matches. If you haven't got glasses, crockery etc ready yet, use paper cups and plates.

If you feel stressed out, don't be ashamed to ask one or two of your best friends to help you. They can take over some of the organising, for example, invite people on your behalf.

It can be a good idea to have a house cleansing ritual before the house blessing ritual. This is sensible if you feel that there are any unpleasant vibes in the house, if you didn't like the people who lived there before you, or there's a room in the house which has a cold or creepy atmosphere.

Talk to your priestess about this. She can suggest and conduct a suitable ritual. This can be held immediately before the guests for the blessing arrive.

Either you, or the priestess, can also dedicate and consecrate your personal shrine or altar before the ceremony, if you wish. I'm not including either the house cleansing or the altar consecration in this ritual, since I feel that they very personal and it may not be appropriate to share with many people. By the way, if a house cleansing and altar consecration is not required, you can ask a crone to take the role of priestess.

Sample Invitation

My sister Elizabeth, Catherine her daughter and Bast and Sekhmet their cats are moving into their new home. They have asked me to invite you to their Home Blessing and House Warming Party on 1 May

The ceremony will be led by the Rev. Angelica of the Fellowship of Isis.

Try to be there at 4pm prompt. The ritual will start with an outdoors procession, so please bring suitable shoes and clothes. It will be followed by a party. Please bring something to eat or drink for sharing.

If you can think of a small meaningful gift, please contact me with your idea, so that I can incorporate it into the ritual.

Please let me know if we may expect you.
Daniela.

What You Need

* Charged water and salt, mixed (supplied by the priestess)

* Candles (in any colour that looks friendly and homely to you)

* Matches

* Incense burner

* Rosemary and lavender incense

* Bells, tambourines, finger cymbals

* Cassette player

* Drinks (alcoholic or non-alcoholic, to be supplied by the guests) Some additional non-alcoholic drinks

* Paper cups and plates (unless you feel they're a waste of resources, in which case you can use proper plates and glasses)

* Rugs and cushions for the guests to sit on (plus a few chairs for the less mobile guests)

* Horseshoe, nails and hammer (Optional:)

* Goddess statue or picture representing the aspects of protector of home, e.g. Vesta.

Gifts

It is customary for guests to present gifts to the hostess. These should include a small container of salt (preferably sea salt) and a loaf of bread (preferably a large flat home-baked wholemeal loaf), a sandtrap, a horseshoe.

You can also include house or garden plants, spices, incense, small decorative items, canned food (people who move home usually deplete their food stores rather than transport them), magical items for protecting the home.

A sandtrap traps negative energy before it can enter the home. This is how to make one. Get a glass jar with a firm stopper, e.g. from a car boot sale, or one which used to hold spices. Collect two different types of sand from two different places. Maybe one from the local beach, and one from the place where you go on a holiday. Hopefully, they have different colours. Put each portion of sand into a small bowl. Touch first one sand, and feel or imagine the energy coming from it, charge it with your own personal power, and say a spell or prayer over it. Pour it into the glass jar until the jar is half full. Then repeat the same with the other sand. Place the lid on firmly. Say 'May this sand trap all malice, violence and ill will so that they cannot enter the house which it will guard. So mote it be'.

A good book with instructions how to make magical protective items which cost little or nothing, and how to charge them, is *'Earth Air Fire & Water'* by Scott Cunningham. Of course, some guests may like to present something of greater monetary value, for example, parents may like to give their daughter an item of furniture when she moves into her first flat.

Body of the Ritual

The guests, lead by the new occupant and the priestess, walk in a procession around the house and gardens. It will probably not be possible to walk exactly along the boundaries of the property, especially not in the case of a terraced house or a bedsit.

Just make all the detours necessary, even if it means walking around half the village. From time to time, everyone should look in the direction of the house, and visualise it as cosy, comfortable and safe.

During this procession, you should play your finger cymbals, tambourines, sistrums, rattles, bells whatever. Make a noise, sing, skip and dance. Depending on the route you are taking, it can be a good idea to tell the neighbours in advance what will be going on, or to cease noise making on certain parts of your route.If you've moved into a very conventional, quiet neighbourhood, don't play the bells and tambourines at all during the procession; carry and wave small branches of trees instead. When the procession arrives at the front door, the hostess or a friend recites this poem:

Moving Home
(by Lawrence Long)

World in motion:
The world is not a stasis
It is a kaleidoscope of
New faces, new places

Hearth is where the heart is
Bless these walls
From tranquillity to parties
When the heart calls

Let the moving of the body
Please not move the mind:
Let us stay kind

Bless this house, its silence and its noise
Its experience of life as well as its joys
May we be good neighbours
May we bring our labours
To help the house to aid us
A happiness in this house
A happiness all around
A blessing and a blessing
Upon this place we've found

Let us pause a moment
Before we make this move
And pray grant the homeless
A roof.

A friend takes the horseshoe and holds it up.

Guest 1:
'*May this horseshoe attract the energy of many horses to this house, entering through the front door.*'

She nails it to the door. (Make sure you have suitable small nails and a hammer at hand.) Some people feel it's luckier to have the horseshoe with the points up, others with points down. Do it whichever way you prefer.

A second friend takes the sandtrap, holds it up.

Guest 2:
'*May this sand trap trap all malice, violence and ill will so that they cannot enter this house.*'

She buries the sand trap, either in soil outside the front door, or in a big flowerpot full of compost. (Make sure a small spade or a flowerpot are at hand).

The hostess opens the door. Everyone takes their shoes off. The priestess leads the way in, followed by the guests.

Once inside, the priestess charges and mixes salt and water. Now she leads the procession. The procession should go clockwise around the home, into and around every room. This route too may require a bit of thought and compromise. The layout of most homes doesn't lend itself to a simple clockwise procession. You may be going through certain rooms more than once. Just make sure that you always walk clockwise, and that you cover every single wall. Avoid walking straight across a room, or counterclockwise. Some rooms (e.g. bathrooms) are so small that only one person can get in at a time, in which case that's just what you do.

During this procession the priestess sprinkles the charged and mixed salt water into every corner of every room. All the others can sing, dance, wave twigs, and play bells and tambourines. Now you all assemble in front of the fireplace (if there is one), or in front of a heater, a cooker, aga, lamp or other source of warmth or light. The hostess sits on one side of it, the priestess on the other.

The hostess lights incense. The herbs rosemary and lavender are particularly useful. Their are for purifying as well as for protection. Their fragrance is light, so you won't have any heady smells interfering with your sleep during your first night in the new home.

Priestess: *'May the Goddess bless this home, that it may always be a place of safety, shelter and comfort, for those who live here and for those who visit.*

70

Everyone: *'Blessed be.'*

Priestess: *'May the Goddess bless this hearth, so that it may always be a source of warmth light and nourishment for those who use it.'*

Everyone: *'Blessed be.'*

Priestess: *'May the Goddess bless the people who live here* [insert names] *and the animals who live here* [insert names]. *May they always find this place a true home.*

Everyone: *'Blessed be.' Priestess: 'May the Goddess bless the people who visit this place as guests. May they always bring peace and joy to this place, and find peace and joy here to take away with them.'*

Everyone: *'Blessed be'. Priestess: 'This home and hearth, and the people who live and visit here, are blessed. Now light the fire.'*

'The hostess lights the fire in the fireplace. If there is no fireplace, she chooses some other action which symbolises the use of the hearth. For example, she could boil some water on the cooker, or turn on the fan heater. Be warned if you are using an aga for the first time: it's neither quick nor easy to get it started. In addition, she can add some candles to add light and atmosphere.

If a guest has brought a poem to recite, a song to sing, or a musical instrument to play, now they can offer their contribution. Here is one suggestion for a suitable short poem:

Haven

(by Carol Ann Bill)

Lord, may this house a haven be
The World outside we leave to thee
Within these walls may we find rest
Our hearts and minds with joy be blessed
And so we ask you Lord above
Enfold this house in peace and love.

Now the guests present the hostess with any gifts they have brought for the home (other than the horseshoe and the sandtrap which are already in place). Where I come from, there's an ancient tradition, still observed today, that friends present bread and water on the first day.

Guest 3: *'We bring you bread. May you never go hungry in this house, never suffer need.'*

Everyone: *'So mote it be.'*

Guest 4: *'We bring you salt. May you never lack life energy.'*

Everyone: *'So mote it be.'*

The hostess takes the bread, and sprinkles some of the salt over it. She breaks it into small pieces, puts them on a plate, and hands them around.

Hostess: *'Please share this gift with me.*

Everyone: *'So mote it be.'*

The following part of the ritual can be amended, according to the gifts presented.

Guest 5: 'We bring you wind chimes. May they ring in the air to keep ill winds away from this home.

Everyone: 'So mote it be'.

Guest 6: 'We bring you this blanket. May it always keep you warm.'

Everyone: 'So mote it be.'

Guest 7: 'We bring you this herb pillow. May it always bring you restful sleep'. Everyone: 'So mote it be'.

Guest 8: 'We bring you this small picture frame. May it always preserve pleasant memories.

Everyone: 'So mote it be.'

Guest 9: 'We bring you this pot of houseleek. May this plant always grow on the roof of your house and protect the building from lightning.

Everyone: 'So mote it be.'

Guest 10: 'We bring you this music cassette. May there always be an occasion for celebrating and dancing in this home.'

'Everyone: 'So mote it be.'

Last guest: 'We bring you all these snacks and drinks [reveals the store of bottles and food contributed by the guests] so that we can have a jolly good party now.'

Everyone: 'So mote it be.

This is quite an informal ending to the ritual part, reflecting some of the improvised and ad-hoc nature of home moving.

Have fun, put on some music, get dancing, do more tambourine playing.

Try to keep one room out of bounds for the party part, so that your pets can have some peace and quiet, because they may feel upset by the move.

By the way.... whatever you dream during your first night in your new home is said to become true. May your dreams be pleasant!

Chapter 6
New Business Blessing

Whether your new business is a big operation with premises and staff, or a hobby you plan to turn into a profitable pastime from your kitchen table, a ceremony gets you off to a good start.

This ritual is inspired by rituals I experienced in Mongolia, where I worked as an editor and helped launch the country's first women's magazine.

The ritual takes place during the morning of the first working day. All the staff are present. You can invite friends, business partners, and well-wishers. It may be a good idea to invite potential customers, too. But they should all fit into one room.

You, the new proprietor, should participate in the ritual, but you must get someone else to lead it. A priestess perhaps, or a crone, or someone who is already running a successful business.

Preparation

Make an infusion of kelp and yellow dock. Scrub the floors with it before you move in. If you have carpets and furniture already in place, rub the doors and door frames with the infusion. It is believed to entice customers with good intentions and spending power to your business. If you have toilets on the premises, close the lids of all the toilets, and ask your visitors to close them after use -otherwise your wealth might literally go 'down the drain'.

You may like to consult a geomancer, a fortune teller or a priestess about the arrangement of the furniture, and about the best starting date for your business. When I lived in China, my friends were particular about which directions the desks and cash tills had to face. And when I helped start a business in Mongolia, my client's main considerations about a start date were not financial calculations or staff recruitment, but the advice of a Buddhist lama, of a shaman and of a street fortune teller.

Generally speaking, a business which opens during the first few days of the month is believed to flourish; opening a business towards the end of the month is said to be risking failure.

What You Need

Keep the decorations simple! You don't want to spend hours tidying up afterwards. However, it is good for your luck if you display any well-wishing cards and messages. There's no need to dress up for the ritual, just wear your ordinary work/ business clothes, but they should be smart and clean.

* A garland, made from flowers or from paper, is placed around the frame of the door which leads to the room where you are holding the ritual.

* One table, preferably covered with a turquoise or green cloth, is set up as an altar, near the entrance to the room

* You need extra chairs for everyone to sit on - place them so that they face the entrance.

* Set one table aside to use as an altar, place it near the entrance to the room.

* Also on the table should be an incense burner with incense (benzoin and cinnamon), already burning at the beginning of the ritual.

* Four green or turquoise candles, arranged in a line.

* Several silver-coloured coins (e.g. 5p-pieces), arranged in a line in front of the candles.

* A pot of basil, also placed on the altar. After the ritual, it should be placed on the cash register or near the door; it is said to attract business.

* Peas in shells

* A bowl full of grain (e.g. rye or rice - but the grain must not be peeled or shelled)

* A few empty bowls

* Sparkling wine, sparkling fruit juice, plain biscuits (e.g. 'morning coffee', 'digestive' or 'rich tea').

* Infusion of kelp and/or yellow dock, with a little salt. If unavailable, use salt water.

* You may like to place an image of the Goddess on the altar, showing her in an aspect that relates to business or wealth, or to the type of product or service your business will offer. If you enjoy research, you'll have great fun finding out about Goddesses and their specialist subjects. Here are just a few ideas:

My favourite Goddess image for a women's business is 'Athena Ergane' which means 'Athena the Working Woman'. She is the patroness of career women, crafts people, and anything to do with hygiene.

The Roman Goddess '*Fortuna*' brings good luck and is also patroness of anything to do with baths.

The Roman Goddess '*Flora*' protects business relating to fruits, cereals, vines and flowers.

Another Roman Goddess, '*Fornax*', will guard over a business that involves ovens or hot meals.

Sarasvati', an Indian Goddess, helps if your business has to do with music, performing arts, dance, education or examinations.

The Egyptian Goddess '*Maat*' protects enterprises related to justice, law and truth.

'*Lasya*' is Tibetan and an appropriate Goddess for businesses relating to beauty.

'*Kamrusepas*' is an ancient Hittite Goddess of healing.

'*Bast*', the Egyptian cat Goddess, helps businesses dedicated to creativity and leisure pursuits.

The Irish Goddess '*Brigid*' is a good patroness if your business involves writing, because she is said to have invented it.

A Mongolian/Tibetan Buddhist form of the Goddess '*White Tara*' was chosen to protect the publishing business for whom I worked as a consultant in Mongolia, because '*White Tara*' is a powerful protectress of women and women's affairs. I was also present at the opening ceremony of a new merchant bank in Ulaan Baatar, which was dedicated to a male God of money, but to my shame, I've forgotten his name.

Body of the Ritual

Lead by the priestess, the participants form a procession and walk once clockwise around the premises (on the inside). The priestess sprinkles the kelp/dock/salt infusion into every corner.

When all rooms have been visited, the procession re-enters the room where the ritual takes place. This time, the priestess enters last. Everyone takes a seat; the priestess stands.

The participants take peas and shell them into the bowls during the ritual - this is believed to bring fortune and profit to the business. The more people do it, the better.

The priestess lights the four candles (and the incense, if this has not been lit). The candles should be in one line.

If you like, you can ask the priestess to begin the ritual with an invocation of the Goddess in the aspect you have chosen. But this is optional, and it will depend largely on the type of people whom you have invited.

Priestess: *'We have come together to support* [name]*'s venture. This is an important and exciting moment for* [name]. *Business is about creativity and productivity, about security and risk, about enjoyment and fulfilment, about freedom and about commitment, about plans and about work. Most of all, business is about money. Every business needs money to operate, and it needs to earn money to provide a living for those who run it, for those who work in it, for those who depend on those running it and working there, and also for their suppliers'.*

She holds the silver coloured coins

*'May money flow. May money flow into this business.
May money grow. May money grow out of this business.*

Money flow. Money grow.
Bring wealth to all'.

'Everyone: *'Blessed be.'*

She places the coins into a bowl or other receptacle, and lifts the pot of basil.

'May luck and good fortune aid this business, doubling the effects of good ideas, thorough planning and hard work'.

She places the basil either near the door, or on the cash register, or back on the altar.

She lifts the bowl with the grain.

'May this business nurture and sustain those who are involved with it. May the business grow, and bring satisfaction'.

Everyone: 'Blessed be'.

The priestess pours the grain over the coins.

'Goddess, 'Bless [name] *in her endeavours. Bless* [names] *who work with her. Bless these premises'.*

Everyone: *'Blessed be'.*

Now the priestess collects the shelled peas in a large bowl.

Everyone who pours their peas into the bowl may add a good wish for the business or for the proprietor. For example:

'May your customers always pay promptly', 'I wish you self discipline and stamina', 'May your suppliers always be reliable', 'May you always be full of creative ideas', 'May the bank grant you the credit you need', 'May you always get good

80

advice', 'May you always be aware of your responsibilities towards your staff'.

Avoid wishes which are harmful to others, so don't say something like *'May all your competitors go out of business'.*

The priestess places the large bowl of peas on the altar.

She takes the bowl with coins and grains, makes a sign of blessing over them, and gives everyone a handful of grains. Participants can take these home; they are going to attract wealth to them, too, albeit in a small way only.

The coins and some grains remain in the bowl in the business for one moon. Then the coins should be given to someone who is destitute (e.g. a homeless person, or an under-funded charity).

Priestess: *'May this business be a good business.'*

Everyone: *'So mote it be'.*

The proprietor opens the bottles and offers the biscuits. Many participants will be working or driving after the ritual is over, so sparkling fruit drinks are a good alternative to wine.

Chapter 7
Letting Go (Divorce)

A divorce is a bit like death. Both are about letting go. Both are about celebrating the conclusion of one phase of life and the beginning of something new, and in both cases, we may not be quite ready and willing yet.

Most established religions don't regard a divorce as something to celebrate. They regard divorce as a mark of failure.

Yes, a relationship has failed, because it is no longer working. But it has also succeeded, because it was working for while it lasted, and we celebrate the conclusion of this period.

We also celebrate the courage to set ourselves and our partner free and to step out into a new phase of life. Ending a relationship is about letting go and about liberation.

But it is also about pain (the end of a relationship is almost always painful) - and about healing (scar tissue will form as soon as you are letting go).

When to do This Ritual

Perhaps you don't need this ritual at all. You may have agreed to stay married for 'a year and a day', or 'nine years'. This time has now arrived, and already you have drifted apart. Neither of you wishes to renew the vows. You have parted ways quietly and peacefully. In this case, it is best not to stir things up, but to go your way. You may like to meet up with your partner to carry out a simple, private ritual, thanking each other and wishing each other well for the future.

However, a full ritual can be immensely helpful if:

> * You both wish to be released from your vows before your term is over, especially if you expected and promised to love each other for a lifetime or for eternity.

> * One of you wishes to hold on to the relationship, or to renew it, and the other does not.

The ritual acknowledges that there is pain, that you are justified in feeling it, and that it takes courage to end a relationship. It confirms that you are free from your commitment to each other, and free to begin something new.

Organising the Ritual

This is a ritual that is best organised by the couple who are ready to split up. It's not something that should be presented to them by outsiders. Of course, as a friend, you may suggest doing a ritual, and offer to assist. But don't force it on them. If you would like to have a ritual, but your partner doesn't like the idea, or isn't available, or maybe you are no longer on speaking terms, then you can do it on your own.

The Role of the Priestess

If you have made a vow to stay together for a specific time, then this is a serious promise. It is not to be taken lightly. You wished and you promised. Once this kind of promise has been made, you can't just take it back. You may realise now that it was a mistake to commit yourself for a lifetime or beyond. But you were warned what the commitment meant, and you had decided to go ahead regardless. You must be prepared for the consequences.

Don't think you can just give your priestess a call and say 'Pat and I are splitting up, can you conduct our divorce ceremony.' The release from the vow is something she will grant only after careful consideration, and with the permission of the Goddess.

The priestess' role is to help you to keep your vows rather than to ignore them. She will almost certainly ask you for several meetings, each of you separately and also together, to challenge and test you. She may set you specific tasks. She may suggest you separate for a specific time, and then try to get together again, even if you have already spent months considering and reconsidering everything. She may suggest that you release each other from your promise of, say, sexual fidelity, but not of your commitment to each other.

If she grants a release from your vows in the name of the Goddess, she will probably tell you what to do to 'make good'. This is a kind of atonement, a price to pay for not keeping your vows. It may be something like planting a grove of yew trees on your field, or working in a shelter for battered women. The priestess acts as a mediator between you and the Goddess. The 'penance' should be something that is acceptable to you, but weighty enough to make up as the price for release from a vow.

Of course, nobody will force you to do what the priestess tells you to. But the Goddess (or the deity in whose presence you made the vow) is unlikely to just let you get away with a reneged vow. If you don't give willingly, she may take something else from you. So it may be wise to accept the 'negotiated penance'. It will certainly make you feel better, since you won't be burdened with guilt. The 'penance' may well be something that ultimately enriches you; it may also occupy your body, mind and spirit constructively during a period when you need this. Trust the priestess and the Goddess whom she represents.

Ideally, the priestess who married you should be the one who grants the separation. She is the one who knows the contents of your marriage vows and the term you committed yourself. She is the one who tested and challenged you before she agreed that you should be joined in marriage. She's the one in whose presence you made your promises. You may well feel embarrassed confessing to her that you have failed, but this is only right. She represents the Goddess to whom you made your vows.

If she's not available, ask another priestess to prepare you, test you, and to preside over the proceedings. You need someone to act as a referee to ensure good behaviour from everyone during the ritual, unless you, your partner, and everyone else are models of patience, tolerance and discipline.

Whom to Invite

The ritual of letting go is an intensely personal one, because of its pain, and because it reveals so much about you. Invite only a small group of people, people whom you like and trust, and who you know will support you. Your partner will bring a small band of supporters as well. You don't have to like them. But all the participants need to accept the purpose of the ritual. Leave out anyone with an aggressive temper, they might be tempted to defend you verbally or physically, and you may find yourself surrounded by two quarrelling and warring parties.

Point out at the beginning of the ritual that it is you and your partner who are separating. The others are there to witness and comfort.

Reducing The Bitterness

Naturally, you feel bitter, hurt, disillusioned, angry, or sad, or a combination of all that. Pain and sadness are actual responses, accept them. They may get stronger, but will gradually ebb when the healing begins. They will not be in your way when you carry out the ritual.

The feeling of disillusion is a useful one, because it will protect you from losing belief in yourself. Anger can be helpful too. It helps to externalise your inner suffering, and can shorten the process of separation. Just don't let there be too much anger immediately before the ritual begins. If the anger gets more than you can bear, than do some vigorous sporting activity.

The most harmful of these emotions is the bitterness. It gnaws away at you and damages your health and your self esteem, and may make it impossible for you to be sincere about the ritual. To reduce the level of bitterness inside you, try the following.

*1. Remove all photos, letters, gifts, souvenirs of and from your partner from your living space. You don't have to destroy them, although you may if you wish. But don't look at them as you collect them. Don't be tempted to re-read his letters, or to let your dreams wander to the happy holidays you had when you come across your photos. Just put them in a suitcase or a box. Remove the box from your living space. Put it in a corner in the attic, or ask a friend or distant relative to keep it for you.

*2. Now surround yourself with things which remind you of happy experiences you had which have nothing to do with your partner. The gold medal you won in a dance competition, the letter from the publisher when your novel was accepted, the necklace of dried flowerbuds your little niece made for you. Look through your photo albums (pre-relationship period only). Pick out photos which represent periods of happiness, or which make you smile. Put them up on the wall. Take the happiest of them to your local copy shop or photo shop and have them enlarged.

*3. Find the memorabilia of long-ago relationships (if you still have them and didn't destroy them in a fit of anger). Nothing is more suited to put a crumbling relationship into perspective than previous relationships. As you look at the photos of a bloke with whom you were passionately in love at one time, you'll think 'I thought I couldn't live without him... I thought I'd die from the pain when he cheated on me... but after a few weeks I didn't even think about him anymore. What did I ever see in him?' Go through all the photos, remember the happy and unhappy times you had with other partners. Read through your collection of love letters if you have it, it is bound to make you smile.

*4. If you have kept an emotional diary in years past, read what you have written about the break up of previous relationships. How did you feel then? What was the worst of it? How long did the greatest pain last? How long did it take until you were able to view others as potential new partners?The process of letting go your current partner, the pattern of pain and loss, is likely to resemble that of previous break-ups. You may discover amazing details that you had long forgotten. For example, that you were not able to enjoy food for three days but were ravenously hungry on the fourth. That you had a craving for the smell of fresh lemon balm. That you needed to listen to music constantly, but could not bear to hear the same tune twice. That you found walks by the riverside soothing. If you know what internal reactions to expect, you are better prepared and can summon the courage. You'll be taking the current relationship and it's loss a little less seriously

Preparing the Ritual

Make yourself comfortable in a nice, warm place, where you won't be disturbed. Wear comfortable, cosy clothes. Place a mug of hot chamomile tea, a butter croissant and a huge bar of chocolate beside you and invite your favourite cat to sit on your lap (or whatever makes you feel really cosy and comfortable).

Take a large sheet of paper, and draw a vertical line so that you have two columns. Write the headline 'good things' in one column, and 'bad things' in another. Then list all the things you liked or disliked about your partner, or about your life together. Take your time.

You should find an equal number of 'good' and 'bad' things. The first things you think of are probably the nasty and cruel things he did to you which led to the break-up. The good things may have to do with the beginning of your relationship. But you can put down anything you like, even the things you never told him annoyed you, such as his habit of cleaning his toenails while watching TV.

Your partner should make an equal list - far away from you. Don't meet to compare notes!

What You Need

For the ritual itself you need a quiet, undisturbed place. You can do it outdoors or indoors. It is best to sit in a circle on cushions on the ground or on the floor, unless of course one of you has difficulty getting on the floor or getting up again, in which case you sit on chairs around a large table, with the couple opposite each other.

Dress smartly. Give as much thought to your 'divorce gown' as you did to your 'wedding gown'. Wear your smartest outfit, or buy a new dress, in a colour and style that suits you. Have a nice hairdo and wear glamourous make-up, if you like. It is important that you feel attractive, and that you look good when you start this new phase of your life. But don't waste a single thought on whether your ex-partner will like the dress. You also need:

* For the altar, choose an image of the Goddess which represents independence, strength, courage, transform-ation or healing. Ask the priestess for her advice on which is most appropriate for your situation.

* Candles and flowers can be any colour which is meaningful to you.

* You may like to use fresh healing herbs to decorate the altar, such as lemon balm which has a wonderfully soothing fragrance.

* Incense is optional. You may like to use healing or uplifting incenses or oils, such as frankincense or bergamot.

* Honey

* Salt

* A cord, about one meter long, preferably black (or the two scarves which were knotted together at your wedding)

* Very strong scissors - try garden shears.

* Two helium-filled balloons

* Drums, tambourines, etc

The Body of the Ritual
(Big ritual with both partners, priestess and witnesses)

Everyone sits in a circle on cushions. Priestess lights candles.

Priestess: *'We have come together to witness the unbinding of the knot that ties [name] and [name] together. They have decided to release each other from their vows. We acknowledge the courage this takes, and we back them up with our love and blessings.*

Everyone: *'Blessed be.'*

Priestess (to the other participants): *'Are you all ready to witness the unbinding of this relationship, and to witness the gifts and pledges made during this ritual, and to accept what is happening, without animosity?'*

Participants: 'We are.'

Priestess (to the couple): *'Are you both willing to behave civilly with each other during this ritual, to treat each other with courtesy and respect, and to leave all animosity outside this ritual space?'*

Couple: *'We are.'*

Priestess: *'Sit down then in our circle, so that our love and support can reach you from all sides. Let us get our drums to raise power.'*

The priestess starts the rhythm. Try using a zaar rhythm if you know it, it is used in the Middle East 'to drive evil spirits away', such as the evil spirits of jealousy, anger or hurt. But any other rhythm is fine, too. Everyone else joins in.

Priestess (takes the bowl of honey and places it on the altar): *'Honey represents the sweetness of love.* [Name] *and* [name] *have tasted the sweetness of love.* (takes the bowl of salt and places it on the altar): *'Salt represents the bitterness of love.* [Name] *and* [name] *have tasted the bitterness of love.*

The priestess binds the cord loosely around the couple's wrists, or, if wedding scarves were used, she binds them around the wrists.If the two hate each other so much that they can no longer stand physical contact, then a long rope can be used instead of a short cord or scarves. She then ties helium-filled balloons to their ankles.

The couple now take turns to say each one good and one bad thing about their relationship. These should be very short sentences, without explanations and without accusation. They are not allowed to interrupt, contradict or comment on each other's statements. Keep going until all is said. It helps to have the list at hand, but if your partner has more to say, you may have to rely on your memory to think of more things. Some new thoughts and memories will come up during the exchange.

Now each participants goes into the circle, sits down by the couple, and makes each of them a verbal gift. For example. '[Name of first partner], *I wish you courage.* [Name of second partner], *I wish you new love.'* Then she retreats to her place in the circle.

Priestess *(to one partner): Are you ready to break what binds you?*

Partner 1: *I am.'*

Priestess: *You made a new pledge to the Goddess. Are you willing to repeat this pledge in front of the witnesses, and to do your utmost to keep it?*

92

Partner 1: *I will. I pledge to the Goddess in front of* witnesses *that I will......* (whatever was agreed with the priestess as a suitable atonement).

Priestess (to the other partner): *Are you ready to break what binds you?'*

Partner 2: *I am. Priestess: You made a new pledge to the Goddess. Are you willing to repeat this pledge in front of the witnesses, and to do your utmost to keep it?'*

Partner 2: *I will. I pledge to the Goddess in front of witnesses that I will......* (whatever was agreed with the priestess as a suitable atonement).

Priestess: *'I have asked the Goddess and she is willing to release you from your vows. I cut the cord that binds yo*u.' (cuts the cord scarf or rope with the scissors)

Priestess (to one partner): *'Are you willing to let go of your partner, to set him free? Are you willing not to interfere with his life, and not to see him for a period of at least a year and a day, and then to be friends afterwards?'*

(to promise not to see each other for a specific time is often the best solution for animosity, possessiveness and jealousy. However, it may be necessary to add something like *'except when meetings are unavoidable in the interest of your children.'* This should be agreed in advance between the partners and the priestess)

Partner 1: *'I am.'*

Priestess: *'Watch then the release.'* (cuts the ribbon that ties the balloon)

Priestess (to the other partner): *'Are you willing to let go of your partner, to set her free? Are you willing not to interfere with her life, and not to see her for a period of at least a year and a day, and then to be friends afterwards? '*

Partner 1: *'I am.'*

Priestess: *'Watch then the release.'* (cuts the ribbon that ties the balloon).

If this ritual takes place outdoors, everyone can watch the balloons fly away in the air. If not, just open the window and give the balloons a toss so that they fly.

Everyone hugs the two ex-partners and says something congratulatory such as *'well done'*, *'I'm so glad for you'* or *'Congratulations'*.

Optional: they give each other one last hug.

More drumming. This can again be a zaar, or a different, happier rhythm.

Priestess: *'May you both find peace, healing and strength, and guidance to new relationships when you choose.'*

'Everyone: *'So mote it be'*.

You can dance, or do a chant, or sing a song together, then part. The separated couple should NOT get together for a 'friendly chat' which might only bring out desires or animosities. Remember your promise to stay apart for a year and a day!

Body of the Ritual
(Small ritual for solo use)

This is a ritual you can use if you want to cut yourself free from a relationship, if your partner doesn't want to participate, and if you don't like the formal or public element of a group ritual.

You need: a helium-filled balloon, scissors, comfortable clothes suitable for the weather, a small object that symbolises your relationship, such as a wedding ring, a small pendant he gave you, a photo. Dress smartly, style your hair, apply make-up if you like. You want to look good. Go to a place where there is a good strong tree standing near water (a pond, a stream, a river, a lake, the sea, a waterfall).

Explain to the tree what you are going to do, and why. Dance around the tree to raise power. Sit down under the tree (or, if it is wet and muddy, lean against it's trunk).

'Tree, I ask you to be my witness as I release myself from YYYY and YYYY from me'.

Tell the tree about your partner and your relationship, alternating 'good' things and 'bad things'.

Then you say *'Goddess, the time has come to end this relationship which has become a burden to me. With your permission, I will unbind myself and him to set us free.*

Tie the balloon to your left wrist (your right wrist if you are left handed). Visualise your partner in the balloon. Say to him: '[Name]. *Thank you for the good things we shared. Time has come for you and me to part. I promise not to attempt to meet you for a year and a day, and thereafter if we meet it shall be as friends. '[Name], I set you free'.*

Cut the cord that ties the balloon to your wrist.

Take the object that symbolises your relationship, go to the water and throw it into the water. This is not the same as destroying your relationship; it is just handing back a gift which has served its purpose (think of the sword Excalibur being returned to the Lady of the Lake).

'Goddess, bless me with your strength, courage and healing, that I may be ready for the next part of my life, that the wounds may heal and leave behind scars but no bitterness, and that I may be ready for new aims and new relationships when the right time comes. So mote it be.'

'The following poem is particularly suited for a solo ritual, although it could be recited at a group ritual, too. Say it aloud, and smile.

Divorce
(by Lawrence Strong)

This is the sundering
Not just of two but of one
There is no sun.

But there may be the moon. Soon.

This is the thundering
Not just of one but of two
There is nothing to do.

But there will be a star
Far
But shining where you are
Shining where you are

The hands fall apart
So does the heart
This is a new start
Take heart
Take care
You were loved there
And will be again
Like sun after rain
That old refrain
But so true of pain
The sea may be full of other fishes
But none of them yet seems delicious
Whether or not it was malicious
I've been there. I send best wishes.

Here's another one you may want to consider. It may be helpful to say this aloud if you feel lonely and are still suffering from the hurt.

Love's No Good Today

She got married some years ago.
Why they broke up nobody knows.
It's just the way life is today.
So they say.

She spends her time in emotional pain.
The future looks grim; there's nothing to gain.
Oh! Love's no good today.

She remembers all the time,
when love was good and life was fine.
Getting married wasn't a whim.
She just knew that she loved him.

When he told her that he had to go
With no explanations, 'cause he didn't know.
He just said 'love's no good today'.
Ooh! Love's no good today.

Though, she remembers all the time,
When love was good and life was fine.
But, just for now, love's no good today.
No, love's no good today.

Even if now her mind's in a mess.
Clutching divorce papers
She's got to get dressed.
But when the pain's subsided, it'll go with the rain.
Someone will love her.
She'll be living again.

Sit near the water, meditating quietly for a few minutes.

Say your own words of thanks to the river, the tree and the Goddess. You may like to go for a walk to enjoy your new freedom.

Chapter 8
Croning
(Women's Maturity Celebration)

The turn of the millennium in our patriarchal society is not the best time and place for a mature woman. She becomes the target of jokes (mother-in-law jokes, for example), of ridicule (that ineffective fussy creature who goes to church on Sundays and bingo on Wednesdays) or of pity ('little frail old women') all based on stupid clichés and hostile stereotypes.

The image of the old woman is an ugly one: hunchbacked, with a big nose, several warts and a shrill noise. In omens, dream interpretations and divining the old woman is often a symbol of 'bad luck'. Why? Probably because men are afraid of powerful women. And a crone is a powerful woman indeed.

Instead of honouring her wisdom, they detest her because she is useless to them. She has lost her 'beauty' (i.e. she no longer conforms to the stereotyped beauty norm created by male demand), she is past sex (according to them), and she no longer fulfils the function of childbearing.

The other side of the coin - the female viewpoint - is that now the woman has reached a phase where she does not need a man any longer to protect and support her while she is giving birth or raising children. Her offspring don't depend on her anymore. In short, she can concentrate on developing her feminine powers.

In many cultures, the position of the crone was an honoured one. She was often the clan leader or chieftain of the tribe, she was eligible as the high priestess to the greatest deity, she may have been the healer or magician of the village, her opinions and advice were sought. Even in some patriarchal societies, for example some American Indian tribes, the council of crones had a right to veto any decisions by the male leaders. Of course, we can only speculate about the position of the crone in earlier societies where women were primarily honoured for their fertility. But in many bronze age cultures the average life expectancy appears to have been around thirty-five, so any woman who lived to reach menopause, surviving several pregnancies on the way, must have been a miraculous achiever and her advice on health matters would have been sought after.

When to Celebrate It

Traditionally, the menopause is regarded as the change from mother to crone. But you may feel that your time has come when the last of your children has left the home, when you've become a grandmother or a great grandmother, or when you retire from work. Or maybe just because you feel like it. If you feel you're a crone at 30, then you are.

Reasons to Celebrate

Becoming a crone means starting a new phase of life. It's a liberation. You are free to lead the life you've always wanted to lead. You can leave most of your responsibilities behind. You don't need to worry any more about what will the neighbours think. You can shed your inhibitions. Do what you've wanted to all your life.

You have acquired wisdom and experience, and you can share it with whom you wish. You are free to learn more, if you want to.

You have concluded the phases of life in which you were responsible for others within the family or the work environment. Now you can live for yourself.

You deserve being a crone.

Now You Are Entitled To...

Do what you like, not what others want you to do. When you reach the crone phase of your life, your dependents are old enough to look after themselves. Oh yes, they might like you to think that they need you - your financial contributions, your babysitting hours. But if you were to die, they'd have to manage without you, wouldn't they? And you deserve some fun.

You'd be surprised how many crones come to my belly dance classes. This is what one crone told me, and her response is typical. *'It's something I've wanted to do all my life, but I was worried about what my parents, my children, the people at work would think about it. Now that I'm seventy, people expect me to sit in a rocking chair and knit. They could just about see me taking up ballroom or sequence dancing. But belly dancing? At my age? They are shocked. But guess what? Now I don't care any more. I'm having fun. I think they are envious'.*

Another crone I know bought herself a boat and spends her life sailing around the world; yet another sold all her belongings and settled down in Thailand.

If you've always felt you missed out on education in your youth, enrol on a university access course and then go and become a student.

Here are some other suggestions:

* Take up a hobby that has always fascinated you, but for which you never had the time or the courage. Acting, singing, calligraphy, oil painting, parascending, circus skills?

* Apply for a volunteer job in a developing country with VSO or BESO. VSO (Voluntary Services Overseas) sends qualified people for two year periods. BES (British Executive Services Overseas) sends highly qualified experts for shorter periods, between three weeks and six months, to train people in developing countries. Both welcome mature applicants, especially women.

* Write that book. If you've always wanted to write a novel, or the story of your own life, now is the time to do it.

* Start a herbarium.

* Train to become a priestess of your religion.

* Start a LETS network in your neighbourhood. LETS stands for Local Exchange Trading System. It's a network of bartering. I give you a belly dance lesson, you do an oil painting of someone else, who in turn mows a neighbour's lawn, and the neighbour does my ironing. All without changing money. These networks work beautifully and it's amazing what you can get without money. But the LETS networks need people like you, who can organise, initiate and motivate.

* Train as a special constable. You can contribute to the safety of the area where you live.

* Learn Reiki and other healing techniques and become a healer. But don't work too hard!

Most people have less spare time than ever before. Really set time aside for your projects, and also for rest. Above all, do what you really like, not what others want. Stop worrying about what others think. You've reached the age of dissent.

It is quite likely that some people will try to make you feel guilty if you refuse to spend your retirement looking after their children and organising the coffee mornings for their charities. Family members in particular tend to view your retirement as their opportunity to acquire an unpaid servant. Tell them cheerfully that you don't have the time to do their babysitting because you are too busy enjoying yourself.

You And Your Body

Your own body. Know what's going on with it, and take an informed decision. Especially regarding Hormone Replacement Therapy, which is either the best thing that's happened to women this century, or the worst, depending on who you're listening to. Listen to both sides, then decide. A good book is Leslie Kenton: *Passage To Power, Natural Menopause Revolution*, published by Vermillion.

Start an exercise programme. Exercise has the following benefits:

* It increases your life expectancy. Scientists estimate that you people who exercise live on average 7 years longer.

* It makes your bones strong. This is particularly important now because your bones could become brittle with age and might fracture easily.

* It gives mental clarity, mental energy, and mental flexibility.

* It fights that feeling of being 'low'

* It helps you relax and have a good sleep

* It strengthcns your immune system

* It keeps your joints supple, improves your stamina and tones the muscles.

Exercise does not have to be tedious. You can do it in the privacy of your home, with an instruction video. Try to choose one whose instructor didn't have her lower ribs removed to achieve that wasp waist, or looks so fit slim and beautiful that you feel substandard.

Videos are great if you wish to exercise in private, but if you want someone to correct and encourage you, and a bit of socialising, you are better of with a weekly class at your gym or adult education centre. You can choose a ladies-only class, a class for the over 50's only, or exercise for the 'unfit' - all of which may make you feel better than a room full of teenagers in competitive spirit.

Dancing is one of the best exercises you can get. Try a dance where you don't depend on a male partner, for example line dancing, circle dancing, flamenco or belly dancing ('raks sharqi' in Arabic). Flamenco and belly dancing especially celebrate the mature woman. They allow you to be passionate and sensuous, powerful and alluring. Personality and expression count for more than a smooth skin.

It's always a good idea to talk to your medical adviser about the exercise programme you are planning. Yes, your doctor may raise an eyebrow if you ask his opinion about belly dancing... and so may your daughter-in-law and your neighbour. But once you've achieved crone phase, you need not let conventions inhibit you. However, listen to medical advice. For example, if you have severe arthritis in your joints, flamenco or Scottish dancing may not be as good as other dances.

Just for your information, I'm teaching belly dancing, and most of my students are 50+, many are in their seventies or eighties. They have much more fun with the dance than the younger ones. You are unlikely to be the only crone in your belly dance/flamenco/salsa/whatever class.

With Whom To Celebrate

It's your women friends who have already reached the crone phase who should organise the party to welcome you to the sisterhood of crones. That's the tradition.But if they ignore your hints and no party is forthcoming, then disregard the tradition and throw your own party.

This is strictly a party for crones, that is for mature women who are mature, old, wise, knowledgeable, and experienced, or possess at least several of these attributes.

You definitely don't want any teenagers or indeed anyone below the age of 26. They don't know how to have fun, they are too inhibited. You don't want any men either; they'd feel threatened.

Try to get at least three women to celebrate with you. Around six is better to create a party atmosphere. You may like to assemble eight or twelve women with you, so that you have the traditional numbers of a witches' coven (9 or 13), and have a coven for a day.

Invitations for a croning party are by word of mouth - don't bother with formal written invitations.

Presents

Every participant gives the new crone a present. These should include:

* A crown. Hand-made from cardboard or papier mache, sprayed with gold and decorated with sequins or fake jewels. Or something bought ready-made from a theatrical shop.

* A golden key, able to unlock untold riches from heaven and earth. Any old key will do, sprayed gold.

* A book with blank pages

Other ideas for gifts are: aids for healing, a book on medicinal herbs, a book on goddesses, books/videos/magazines relating to the new activities the crone plans, or about healthcare and spiritual wellbeing.

In addition, everyone contributes a piece of 'wisdom', e.g. tips about herbs and healing, about feng shui or magic.

Dressing Up

Every crone should have a special crone's dress. This should be the dress of your dreams. YOUR dreams, not your daughter's or husbands dreams! They will never see it. The only people who will ever see it are the crones. Yes, you've guessed correctly. It's a dress which makes you feel fabulous, confident and careless. It should be extremely comfortable, it should make you look good (by your standard, not anybody else's).

The traditional colour for crones is black. Black in this context symbolises maturity, completion, depth and mystery.

Unfortunately black is also a conventional and dull colour. So if you choose black, brighten it up. But you may prefer a colour which makes you feel confident.

Make your own gown, commission a seamstress, ask your mother to make it, buy it from a charity shop, rummage through jumble sales, raid your fancy dress box, whatever. Then add decorations. Embroider, sew and glue them on. Textile glue is a fabulous invention for those who hate needlework. Try to get textile glue which is washable. Fabric paint which comes in tiny bottles is also perfect for giving your creativity free flow. Paint swirls, five pointed stars, ankhs or butterflies in your favourite colours. Fabric paint is now available with tiny bits of glitter mixed in, which gives sparkly effects. Coins, old buttons, beads, single earrings, bits of broken fashion jewellery, curtain fringing, feathers, Indian mirrors, tassles, holographic sequins... you like it? Go for it.

Don't let anyone interfere with your creative flow. The only rule is: your gown must be unique!

You Need:
Have the presents for the new crone ready.

Full bodied red wine, mature cheese, and other foods. Choose foods which don't require cooking, and which you would not normally eat. Caviar, perhaps?

Depending on the entertainment you choose, you may need a cassette player or craft materials.

You don't need an ordained priestess for this ritual. Every crone present is a priestess in her own way. Room decorations are unimportant. Decorate yourself instead.

You can use candles and incense if you wish. Sage and frankincense are good incenses for this ritual. You may also like to place bunches of fresh herbs in the room. These will obviously depend on the season, but I suggest sage and lady's mantle.

Body of the Ritual

All sit in a circle, either on cushions or on chairs.

You may like to begin with an invocation of Hecate, the holy crone, but this is optional.

First crone: *'We have come together in this circle to welcome* [name] *into the sisterhood of crones, the coven of the ancient wisdom of the ancient women.'*

Second crone: *'We have come together to value experience, our own and that of other crones, to share what we have learnt.'*

Third crone: 'We *have come together to remember together the crones that were before us, the stories of women's lives,* our own and those of our ancestors.'

Everyone: *'So mote it be'*

First crone: *'You have completed a large part of your life cycle, and you have achieved an incredible lot in this short time, for example* [name some of her achievements, e.g. having brought up three children, having passed an educational exam, having learnt to swim]. *You are a queen among women. You deserve the golden crown.'*

(places the crown on the new crone's head).

Second crone: *'You have gained wisdom through your own experience. You have learnt from your own mistakes, and from*

your successes. We give you this golden key. It will unlock the wisdom within you, and the wisdom from other sources, which you can use for your own benefit and the benefit of others.'
(Presents the key to the new crone)

Third crone: *'Your life is a book of stories. Stories of hopes and ambitions, of successes and disappointments, of love and longing, of frustration and of joy, of duty and honour. It is a book of stories as old as time, experienced by thousands of women in all ages, of stories as new and fresh as only you yourself have experienced them, of stories shared and of stories kept secret for ever. We give you this book in appreciation of the stories you have lived, and the stories you are going to live.*
(Presents the book to the new crone)

Now each crone tells a story from her own life, or from the life of an ancestress. The new crone is the last to contribute a story.

Then one of the crones recites this poem:

A Passage of Time
(by Linda Vincent)

As a young child she would stumble and fall,
But she took life as it came, intrigued by it all.
Then she grew into a young girl full of life with complex schemes
Her world a changing pattern, her future a batch of dreams.

As teenage years drifted by, loves were won and lost.
She learned the art of compromise, sometimes to her cost.
But life made a woman of her. She became so many things.
From a daughter to a lover, now she wears a wedding ring.

Her body went through changes, she began to bloom and grow.
She felt a life inside her, that no man would ever know.
Then her children left the nest that she had made with pride.
Sometimes memories were painful things, but she hid the tears she cried.
Edging to her autumn years she tells the child that grew,
Of all the wondrous things in life that only women knew.
Another name adorns her life and that is as a Nan.
With grandchildren all around she relives her childhood plan.

This has been her passage of time from which she has stood the test.
Of all the ways to travel this world it's women who have the best
For you can be sure; of this, there is no doubt.
'They get to know through being what life is truly about.

Now each crone presents the new crone with a piece of wisdom and advice. Perhaps recipe how to make a herbal remedy, or a spell to ease arthritis. It is a good idea to have the advice written down as well, so that the new crone can refer to it when she needs it. The new crone recites one of the following poems:

Maturing
(by Lawrence Long)

I am no longer subject to the blood
I am loosening ties
I am wise

I have fulfilled or not fulfilled, as the case may be
But it is not just the next generation that has a future
I breathe the air of liberty

I breathe it down by the sea
Waving goodbye to the moon and tide
I enjoy the seaside

I feel both wise and reckless
Like a woman who buys a necklace
Called the future
And it suits her
And it suits me, this liberty
The return of equality
In this sorority

Give blessings for what has passed
Give blessings for what is near
Give blessings for the rest
Give blessings for what is here.

Cerrídwen
(extract from a poem by Kazz)

My Lady I see you
Standing amidst a clearing
Within your sacred Grove
In green and purple clothed.

At your feet a blackened cauldron
Bubbles as you stir,
Golden bubbling laughter
Ready to flow over.

Without hesitation I come to help you stir
Bright and golden elixir
We stir my lady's brew.

The Entertainment

Croning shouldn't involve a traditional meal. On this occasion, nobody should be bothered with chores such as peeling potatoes or washing up. In a restaurant, the atmosphere would be too formal, and in a pub you couldn't behave as outrageously wicked as you like because people are watching.

Instead, put together some snacks which suggest ripeness, maturity and joy of life. Go to the delicatessen and get a selection of unusual mature cheeses. Add crackers, some juicy strawberries, and round it off with a bottle of full bodied wine of the 'aged in old oak casks' variety.

The entertainment should be enjoyable. It can be reflective, educational and inspiring, or outrageously wild and wicked. This is YOUR party!

Here are some suggestions:

* Get a speaker who can give you tips how to take care of your body (e.g. a herbalist or nutritionist)

* Get a beautician to show you make-up tricks in your home

* Get a colour consultant to show you the colours which make you look vibrant and beautiful

* Book a flamenco or belly dance instructor for a one-hour workshop

* Get a professional storyteller to weave a tale 'Once upon a time, there was a crone...'

* Do your own story telling

* Book a male stripper and insist that the agency sends their most talented artiste

* Practice scrying with a crystal ball, a pendulum, tea leaves, molten lead and other methods you've never tried before

* Try out some magic spells

* Decorate a cape or cloak for the new crone to wear over her gown

* Practice African drumming with big djembe drums.

Chapter 9
Passing Over
(Mourning and Memory Celebration)

Why We Celebrate

To celebrate a death may seem strange, even offensive, in a society where the passing away of a person means a loss, and an occasion for mourning. Most of us put enthusiasm and effort into christenings (or the pagan equivalents), weddings and other rites of passage. Shouldn't we put equal thought, enthusiasm and effort into celebrating someone's passing over? Shouldn't funeral parties be enjoyable and stimulating events? True, it if someone leaves it can be a loss, and yes, grief is a natural and worthy reaction.

But death is also an achievement, a conclusion, a cause for celebration. All rites in this book celebrate the passing from one phase of life to the next one. Death is the most fundamental of these changes, because it concludes a whole life. It is also the most uncertain, because nobody knows what the next phase will be like, although many of us have clear beliefs.

All religions emphasise that there is a new life after death. They just disagree on what it is like, where it takes place, and how we get there. Even atheists cannot but agree that our bodies, once dissolved into particles, are fed into the cycle of life again. It is the uncertainty, combined with our personal loss, that makes us feel the grief.

The person who died has departed for a long journey to a destination where she has never been before.

If you feel pain and fear on her behalf, compare her journey to an adventure trip on this planet. Imagine her having set off to work her way around the world, or to climb a mountain in the Himalayas, or to explore the Brazilian rain forests. You would feel worried but thrilled for her, maybe a little bit envious; you would light candles and pray for her or cast a spell for strength and protection.

By dying, she has gone maybe on a long and hazardous journey, so we gather to wish her a safe journey, and to give her a farewell dinner and maybe presents.

Organising The Funeral

Conventional funeral rites have grown from the Christian religion and draw heavily on traditions form the Victorian era. They can be meaningful and soothing to some, yet painful, alienating, embarrassing to others.

The law does not force you to have a funeral carried out in this way. Actually, there's a lot of freedom to organise the event creatively, but this is not always easy.

This book deals with ritual and it is not possible to look in great depth at the organisation of a D.I.Y. funeral. If you want really practical advice, here are two excellent books: *Sue Gill and John Fox, The Dead Good Funerals Book,* published by Engineers of the Imagination. *The Natural Death Handbook,* published by Virgin Books. These books will tell you everything you need to know.

But while you are considering the options, here are some pointers:

* Using the services of a professional funeral director can take the strain away from the event. The undertaker has the experience and knowledge to make things run smoothly, and is also experienced at dealing with grief. It is a good option if you don't want hassle, if money is no major problem, and if you want a conventional funeral. Some funeral directors are also willing to organise 'alternative' funerals. However, they are in the business of making money, and naturally they want to sell extras to make a profit. They need to earn a living, pay their staff and their overheads. You should not scorn them for that. To avoid being overcharged, simply 'shop around', contact several funeral directors and compare prices.

* Organising a D.I.Y. funeral is probably less costly. Some activities involved - such as tucking the body in, shovelling the earth, lowering the coffin - can help friends and relatives to accept their grief positively. But it is not suitable for everyone. If something goes wrong due to inexperience, it can be devastating.

* You don't need to buy an expensive wooden and varnished coffin. Flat-packed bio-degradable coffins are available. You can paint them with meaningful scenes and symbols. Or you could get an artist to turn the coffin into a work of art.

* You could also follow pre-coffin traditions and wrap the body in a woollen shroud (blanket).

* Funeral directors usually supply (at a cost) a special burial suit or gown in which the deceased looks smart and dignified. But you could have your friend wear her favourite dress or casual wear, or their ceremonial robe.

* Your friend does not need to be buried in a cemetery with a conventional grave stone. It is possible to bury someone in a field or in a garden, as long as the owner gives permission. However, the property value may fall if there is a grave in the garden, and if you plan several graves in one place it may need planning permission as a cemetery. You can plant a tree above the grave.

* Some local authorities have set aside woodland sites for alternative burials.

* A burial costs probably less than a cremation.

* A burial at sea is fraught with so many rules, regulations and restrictions that it has become nearly impossible.

* Embalming can be sensible if the body has to be transported over a long distance, if the family wish to view the body, if there is a risk of infection, or if the deceased always wanted to look good. It smoothes out the wrinkles and makes the face look more colourful and alive. However, environmentalist are concerned that the fluids and processes used are damaging to the environment.

Why A D.I.Y. Funeral May Not Be Possible

There are many reasons why a funeral may be conducted in a manner that's against your, or your departed friend's wishes.

First of all, there is the hurry. You can't keep a dead body waiting for a long time, and if the death was unexpected, it can be difficult to find the time to organise a complex ritual. Your mind may be numbed by grief, and you cannot rally the strength to arrange things.

There may be pressure from conventional-minded people, who insist that things are done the 'proper' way. Grieving family members may find a traditional funeral soothing and out of respect for them you give in. You may not be present at the funeral at all, perhaps because you are currently abroad, or your friend was actually on another continent when she died and is being buried there. Perhaps you have been deliberately excluded from the funeral celebrations - for example, because you, the lesbian lover of many years, have in their eyes no right to be there, while the long estranged husband by name only has.

If any of these things have happened and the funeral has left you unsatisfied, or you feel that your dead friend will be unsatisfied by it, just hold your own celebration with a group of friends. It can fill that spiritual void and soothe away the bitterness.

Whom To Invite

You may like to invite just a few close friends, or you may open your house to everyone who knew your dead friend - it's up to you. A small party is certainly easier to organise and control. An open house however can be a generous gesture after a funeral; you invite everyone who attended the funeral to the party. Just explain what you intend to do, then everyone can decide for themselves if they wish to join a celebration under your direction or not.

In either case, it helps if you let people know in advance what you plan to do, with a brief outline about the ritual. If they know what to expect, they will probably appreciate the thought behind it, and are not likely to be shocked or offended.

You can issue written invitations, or, if there isn't the time, give people a ring. What you need to tell them is:

* When and where to meet

* Whether there will be food

* What to wear - respectful mourning clothes or cheerful party wear?

* What to bring - contributions to food & drink, gifts for the dead, flowers, decorations, poems, photos?

* A summary of the ritual

* Optional: a mention of your friend's after-life beliefs, which will make it easier for the guests to understand certain rituals

* whether the invitation is for them personally, or if they may bring their children and friends

Sample Invitation

Dear Friends,

To celebrate Jacintha's completion of her life, and to wish her a good journey to the Otherworld, we will have a passing over party.

Meet at 1pm at our home. We will enjoy a hearty vegan meal. Julian has prepared a slide show of all the stations of Jacintha's life for us all to view. We will follow this with a ritual with candles, directed by Lois. Please bring a candle. We would welcome any story, poem, song, dance or painting you wish to contribute.

As a memorial to Jacintha, we will plant an oak tree and a climbing rose in the garden, and maybe dance around them. If you can play a musical instrument, please bring it with you.

Please wear smart casual clothes, and bring outdoor shoes - the garden tends to be muddy at this time of the year.

Elizabeth

The Funeral Meal

In the area where I come from - the Southwest of Germany - there is the tradition of the 'Leichenschmaus'. This sounds macabre and cannibalistic, translated it means literally 'corpse feast'. But it is simply a hearty meal enjoyed after the funeral. In the old days, it was often a marvellous occasion to make new acquaintances and to renew old ones, and many a young woman met her future husband at a Leichenschmaus. These days the hosts provide just a cup of tea for everyone, which is a dismal affair, and mean compared with the old generosity.

Customs of funeral meals can be found in the traditions of many cultures, and some still take place. This is sensible, just think about it. Something to chew, something hot in the stomach, is always soothing and takes away some of the pain. Food is a symbol for life, and eating shows in a practical manner that life goes on.

So what do you serve? It doesn't really matter, as long as it is hot. Unless you really enjoy cooking and find it a soothing activity, stay clear of elaborate meals. A five course meal for twenty-four guests may be more demanding than you are up to just now. Baked beans and chunks of bread are just fine. They fill the stomach and warm the soul. Incidentally, beans stand as a symbol for the connection with the underworld, and have a long tradition as food at funeral services. In ancient Rome, beans were served at funeral meals and distributed to mourners. If you want something more sophisticated, use a catering service.

122

There's a strange custom observed in several countries (but not as far as I remember in Southwest Germany), that you should not use knives when eating. The reasoning is that the departed's spirit may still be hovering around the place and you might accidentally cut it.

According to some traditions, you should call the deceased's spirit to join you, to give it some food, and also to call and feed other hungry spirits who were not fed by their own mean relatives. Other traditions say that it is cruel to call back those who have just started out on their new journey, because it might confuse them about where they belong. It's difficult for us to know what's right - so maybe we should leave it to the spirits to decide if they wish to join the party.

What You Need For The Ritual

* Food, crockery, cutlery (minus knives?), enough chairs for the meal

* Flowers to decorate the room. Fresh flowers are best; they add life.

* Plenty of candles. Candles lend a quiet dignity to this event. Don't forget candlesticks and candle holders.

* A table or box, covered with a nice cloth, to act as altar

* Any decorations you wish to add. Making decorations can be a good way to occupy grieving children sensibly. The three colours are black (for grief, and for absorption of life and power), white (for light and new beginnings, like a blank canvas), and green (for everlasting life and growth).

* Optional: statues or pictures of the Goddess in her aspect of death and afterlife (such as Nephtys, Persephone, Amentet) or of the deity in which your friend believed.

* Large sheets of paper (bits of wall paper?), pens, pencils, crayons, watercolours

* A box for offerings (cardboard, wood, metal, whatever).

* A plant (this could be herb seeds to grow on the windowsill, or the departed friend's favourite tree to plant in the garden

* At least one spade.

* Twigs of cypress (if available)

* If you want to use incense, I suggest cypress incense or oil. The fragrance of the cypress is wonderfully calming and strengthening in times of crisis. It is not a 'happy' incense, but it can lift the feeling of depression, and ease excessive grief. Or try myrrh.

The Mistress of Ceremonies

Appoint someone to guide the assembly through the ritual - normally this will be an ordained priestess or priest. But you can ask someone else to take on this role, especially if you can't get hold of a priestess at such short notice.

It is best if this is someone who has experience in conducting ceremonies, or in public speaking, or as a professional entertainer. An inexperienced guide might falter under the weight of her own feelings and grief, and this would lead to embarrassment.

It is wise if the mistress (or master) of ceremonies is NOT a close friend or relative, so that she or he can remain calm and detached enough to carry the ritual through even when everyone else is sobbing. Someone who has known, appreciated and respected the person, without emotional involvement, is probably best.

Body of the Ritual

Feel free to alter and adapt this ritual to fit in with your, and your departed friend's religious beliefs and with the circumstances and personal preferences.

Everyone is seated at the table.

Mistress of ceremonies: *'This is a ritual of passing for* [name], *who was born on....... in..... and has died on..... in....* [name] *has departed for the Otherworld before us. We wish her a good journey.* [Name], *if you wish to join us in the celebrations in your honour and memory, we welcome your presence among us.*

The priestess passes the food and drink to the person on her left, so that the dishes and bottles circulate the table clockwise, while everyone helps themselves.

Priestess: *'Goddess, bless this food and water. Thank you.'*

'Everyone eats.

When everyone has eaten, the priestess says: *'Goddess, we thank you for the meal in memory of* [name], *and ask your blessings for those who have stayed behind. Blessed be.*

'Everyone: *'Blessed be.'*

'The mistress of ceremonies leads the party to where the main part of the ritual takes place and explains what is happening.

The hostess plays quiet, slow (but not depressing) music. Everyone takes a candle, places it in a candlestick, lights it, and carries it to the altar, then says the words:

'I will remember Jacintha for her sense of humour (or, her dancing skill, her energy, her wisdom, her mince pies, her healing, her generosity, her understanding, her sparkling 'eyes...) and I give her this picture (poem, flower, knife, cooking spoon, knitting yarn...) *for her journey.'*

The gift is also placed on the altar.

One after the other steps forward, places the candle on the altar, says what they remember her for, and add their gift. There is no censorship on what they liked her for, or on the suitability of gifts. The givers need not explain. What seems trivial can have a deep symbolic meaning.

The priestess now calls on the people who wish to recite a poem, sing a song, perform a dance, present a slide show, or do something else in the departed's memory. These could be their own words and compositions, or something created by someone else but which touches them.

Here are three poems, published with the writers' kind permission:

Loved One
Angela Harrison

Oh loved one...
You will be sorely missed on this earth
You brought us all such joy and mirth

126

And although it is so sad for us to say "farewell"
We know in our hearts
Where you are going the angels dwell

And as you pass through the gateway to the other side
Be sure they will greet you
And fill your heart with pride
So fear not, loved one
Remember you we always will

And as we all unite together, here today
Your presence and precious memories
Will remain with us forever, all the way
And like a ship that goes out with the tide
We have faith and know
You will always be by our side

Love Is The Shining Light
Carol Ann Bill

Close your eyes, still your heart,
See a shining star
See it shining everywhere
Near and oh so far
Feel it's rays reach out to you
Warm and full of love
Feel the power of God within
Peaceful like a dove.

In our hearts there burns a light:
Love - and it grows bright
Till one day we love so much
Our hearts as one unite.
Give your Love to all mankind
Take Love in return
For the power of Love is true

That's something we must learn.
Life eternal, life divine
Love transcends all time
Death is but a step beyond to freedom, peace of mind.
When God takes those dear to us into this world so bright
We shall reach them through our Love.
Love is the shining light

(If you like, you can SING this poem. The writer wrote the words to go with the music of Dvorak's 9th (New World) Symphony, the same piece of music that has been played to the Hovis adverts)

Land of Summer
Sarah Rooke

Strong, fragrant incense fills my heart
I have left this Earth plane on a cloud marked 'mine'
I can see it in your eyes
That we will never be far apart
I shall follow the Stars Say
'Farewell to thee' of this mortal coil
Head for the Spheres, Beyond the limits of our bodily toil
As my Spirit and Soul breaks free
Know then there is no need to grieve
For I have found the Land of Summer.
That point as the sign into Blessed Life

Passing Over
Lawrence Long

We all desire to be accomplished
And now this is accomplished
Thank you for the pleasure of your days
Thank you for the measure of your ways

Thank you for what everyone remembers.
Laughing Junes, festive Decembers
Thank you for your anecdotes and jokes
For the times with the ladies and the blokes
Thank you for the pleasure of your rounds
Thank you for the pleasure of your sounds
Thank you for your friendliness and care
Thank you for the clothes you used to wear
Thank you for your company at meals
For saying things that everybody feels
For the care you showed towards your family
For being the way a friendship ought to be
Thank you for your hobbies and your style
Thanks for sharing in so many a mile

They say you're moving further down the road
I'll see you there when I've put down this load.

(If you like, you can personalise this poem. For example, say
'your music' instead of 'your hobby', or 'the woolly hats you
used to wear' instead of 'the clothes you used to wear'. This
poem may help everyone to smile and feel grounded.)

After these performances, the priestess explains activity
which uses creativity and memory. For example, she places
large sheets of wallpaper and crayons on the table, and
everyone paints memories and good wishes.

Or a member of the family may have prepared a poster with
photos of the departed person, or a slide show of her life,
which can be presented to the audience, with explanations.

The priestess thanks everyone for the contributions. She
extinguishes the candles and gathers the gifts from the altar,
into a box or bag. She leads the party into the garden (if there
is one!).

Priestess: '[Name], *we present you with this box. It contains our gifts, for you to remember us by, and to help you on your journey to the Otherworld.*

'Party guests dig a hole in the earth, which needs not be wide but it must be fairly deep, and place the box into it. Then they throw some earth on it.

The Hostess, aided by party guests, plants a tree (or a shrub, or a perennial flower plant, or even simple grass seeds - whatever is practical and would have been appreciated by your departed friend).

Priestess: '[Name], *we are planting this tree, to remember you by. This will be your memorial in our lives in this world. May this tree grow to give joy and life and peace to all creatures who visit it. So mote it be.*

'Everyone: *'So mote it be.*

If there is are any musicians - amateur or professional - among the guests, it can be dignified and uplifting if they play their instruments. Everyone else holds hands in a circle around the memorial tree and walks or dances clockwise. If you were able to obtain small twigs of cypress, you can give each participant a twig to wear. Chanting and singing are also possible, but give some thought to suitable songs. The departed friend's favourite songs are probably the best choice.

Hostess: '[Name], *we wish you a good journey. Take our blessings with you. Thank you, everyone, for joining us in this memorial party'.*

Mistress of Ceremony: *'Blessed be'.*

Everyone: *'Blessed be.'*

Chapter 10
Creating Your Own
Rituals

Ideas For Many Other Occasions

If you are a creative person, why not create your own
ritual?Close your eyes. Use your vivid imagination to
visualise the event. Where does it take place? Who is present?
What are people wearing? How is the room decorated? What
are people doing? Is there music? Dancing?

Jot down your ideas. Then sort them into 'practical' and
'impractical'. Arrange the practical ones into a sensible order.
Write out a script, so that you don't forget what to do during
the ritual.There are many times in your life when a ritual can
be helpful, or just enjoyable.

Here are some ideas:

Examinations

For most people, the evening before an examination is a
nerve-wrecking time. Your adrenalin level is high with
excitement. You are too nervous to benefit from last-minute
study, yet unable to think of anything else. A quiet ritual is
often the answer. It focuses the mind and gives you calm and
confidence. You might like to invoke a Goddess of learning or
examinations, such as Brigid or Sarasvati. If you are very
nervous, incorporate some physical activity, such as

drumming, brisk walking or dancing. It will make you feel better. You could also bless a small object which you then carry in your pocket for the exam. Whenever you get tense and stuck during the exam, you feel the object, and you feel the reassurance and calm coming from it.

Starting a New Job

Involve a typical 'tool of the trade'. You may like to do it on your own, or with your new colleagues, or with friends. Be a bit careful about inviting new colleagues; you don't know them well, and they may not appreciate the idea of a ritual. If colleagues are involved, it is customary to provide them with cakes or a meal. Say aloud what your hopes are for the new job, what you think you will enjoy doing. If you are carrying out the ritual alone, you can also voice your fears. Ask the Goddess to bless you and protect you.

Going To College/University

Involve a typical 'tool' of your studies, whether this is a text book, a pen, or specialist equipment. Invite people who have been to school with you, as well as friends. You can invite fellow students if you know them. This ritual tends to involve loud music and beer, so choose a venue where your late night partying does not upset neighbours, and try to offer overnight accommodation to your guests so that they don't need to drive home. You could ask them to bring their own sleeping bags. If you like, you and your friends can make really weird decorations. For example, if you are going to study biology, you could decorate the room with giant paper spiders, beetles and paper flowers.

Launching A Creative Project

Perhaps you have choreographed an evening of dances for yourself and your dance troupe. Or you may be an artist and you are opening your first major exhibition. You may be giving a concert, or directing a play. Perhaps you've just had a book published and want to celebrate this success. There are many occasions when you may be presenting the fruits of your creativity and labour to an audience. The success of the project and the audience's response to it are vital.

Your ritual will serve several purposes:

* To calm your nerves before the event by focusing your energies

* To attract audiences to your art project

* To enable you to present the project the best of your abilities

* To create a good atmosphere, positive 'vibes'.

Here you have two choices: You can carry out the ritual quietly on your own, just before the public are allowed to enter. Make sure you secure a quiet and undisturbed half hour, when you are alone with your art. This quiet time is difficult to arrange. Just before the event, there are likely to be all sorts of interruptions, queries, last-minute-arrangements and trouble shooting. This quiet ritual can involve an invocation of the Goddess, asking her to be present, to inspire you and to give you strength and powerful presentation. You may like to dance around the room (clockwise), perhaps singing, chanting, ringing bells, drumming, whatever.

Or you can involve the public. Perhaps your show compere or the sponsor can lead the ritual, beginning with a short speech. You can explain about your art project. Think of ways in which you can involve the audience actively.

If you wish to use incense, use it sparingly. Not everyone likes it. It may enhance the atmosphere for you, but it can give a headache to other people. I've visited a good many creative projects, especially dance shows, and I found the overdose of incense suffocating and off-putting.

Asking For Conception

If you wish to have a child, you may like to carry out a small private ritual - maybe with your partner present - asking the Goddess to bless you with a baby. Eat eggs and dates to symbolise fertility; share them with your partner if you like. There are many fruits, vegetables and flowers which are meant to enhance fertility, some by eating or drinking, others from carrying or smelling. You can place them on the altar. These include: cucumber, carrot, fig, grape, date, olive, hazel nuts (and other nuts), pomegranate, peach, sunflower, poppy, cyclamen, daffodil, geranium, hawthorn, mistletoe, myrtle, and oak. Take your pick. These traditions stem from the times when fertility was a major concern for many couples. Think of those who asked, a long time ago, for the same blessing as you do now.

Pregnancy

With this ritual, you ask for a safe journey for your child, and for health and wellbeing for yourself. Invite several mature women who have given birth and brought up children. Let them touch your belly and bless you. You can also invite your partner, and your existing children. You can include some soft, gentle dancing.

Initiation / Dedication

If you wish to dedicate yourself to a religion, a Goddess, or spiritual path, find out as much about the subject as possible. It is always a good idea to make the first self-initiation for a limited time only, say, for a year and a day. Promise the Goddess (or other deity) that you will dedicate the next year and day to learning about her and from her. Once this initial period is over, you can then choose to dedicate yourself for the rest of your life (or for eternity).

If your path is the same as, or similar to, the path represented by an existing religion or organisation, you should model the ritual on their rites. These are tried and tested rituals, don't reject them. Adjust them as necessary, but use the main elements.

Think carefully about your reasons for choosing self-initiation rather than initiation within an existing body, organisation or group. You may pledge yourself to a path you don't know enough about, or which is unsuitable for you. If you have applied to an existing organisation for initiation, and they turned you down, then they probably had a reason. Perhaps they felt that the path was not right for you, or you were not right for that path. As seasoned practitioners, they probably based their judgement on experience. Think about this; approach another organisation; find yourself an independent teacher and guide if necessary. Don't just rush into self-initiation if group initiation was not possible.

Even if you wish to be a solo practitioner, it can be a good idea to have a sponsor who participates in your ritual. This would be someone of the same, or similar, belief and practice.

They will examine your motivation, perhaps set you a course of study, and they will initiate you at your request. Solo rituals can be sensible if your belief and path are so highly individual that there is no organisation that represents similar paths. You need to be, in effect, priestess and worshipper, teacher and student at the same time. You need to be self-disciplined, and able to set yourself a course of study as well as a moral framework within which to operate. The ritual will probably take place outdoors. Wear a special garment, and perhaps a special piece of jewellery. Take your ritual tools with you.

Recommended Reading

Here are some of my favourite books, which you may find helpful for embellishing my rituals or creating your own, as well as for practical advice on related matters.

Many of them are published in the USA, but are easily available from bookshops in the UK. The older books can usually be found through a book search; ask at a good second hand book shop.

Jacqueline Memory Paterson, *Tree Wisdom*, The definitive guidebook to the myth, folklore and healing power of trees,Thorsons, 1996.

David Conway, *The Magic of Herbs*, Readers Union, Newton Abbot, 1976.

Diane Stein, *Casting the Circle - A Women's Book of Ritual*, The Crossing Press, Freedom, California, 4th printing, 1996.

Scott Cunningham, *Cunningham's Encyclopedia of Magical Herbs*, Llewellyn Publications, St Paul, Minnesota, 1997.

Kris Waldherr, *Embracing the Goddess Within*, Beyond Words Publishing, Hillsobro, Oregon, 1997.

Scot Cunningham, *Earth, Air Fire & Water, More Techniques of Natural Magic*, Llewellyn Publications, St Paul, Minnesota, 1995.

Robin Skelton, *The Practice of Witchcraft Today, An introduction to beliefs and rituals of the old religion*, Robert Hale, London, 1988.

Dolores Ashcroft-Nowicki, *The Ritual Magic Workbook*, The Aquarian Press, Wellingborough, 1986.

Ellen Evert Hopman, *Tree Medicine, Tree Magic*, Phoenix Publishing Inc, Washington, 1991.

Elizabeth Villiers, *The Good Luck Book*, T. Werner Laurie Ltd 1923 (re-published in paperback by Senate, 1994).

Nancy Blair, *Goddesses for Every Season*, Element, Shaftesbury, 1995.

J.C. Cooper, *The Aquarian Dictionary of Festivals*, The Aquarian Press, 1990.

Olivia Robertson: *The Isis Wedding Rite*, The Fellowship of Isis, Enniscorthy, Ireland.

Sir James George Frazer, *The Golden Bough, A Study in Magic and Religion*. This book has been published in a variety of full-length and abridged versions. The original is 12 volumes long and was published from 1890 to 1915. Mine is the abridged version published by Macmillan, London, 1929)

Ernest Crawley, *The Mystic Rose, A Study of primitive Marriage and of Primitive Thought in its Bearing on Marriage*, Spring Books, London, MacMillan, 1902 (various revised later editions were also published)

Leslie Kenton, *Passage To Power, Natural Menopause Revolution*, Vermillion.

Sue Gill and John Fox, *The Dead Good Funerals Book, Engineers of the Imagination.The Natural Death Handbook*, Virgin Books.

Anna Franklin & Sue Philips, *Pagan Feasts*, Capall Bann

Music

I find the catalogue of ARC Music Productions inspiring. Their cassette *'Where Africa meets the Orient'* contains a beautiful song *'Mabrouk Mubrouk'* which is a congratulatory song, suitable for many occasions, and very nice for dancing in a circle.The cassette *'Modern belly dance from Arabia'* contains the famous *'Zeffat Al Aroussa (Bride's Procession)'*. A special wedding dance is also contained on the cassette *'Spiritual belly dance'* ARC Music also have Celtic music and music from other parts of the world, and inspirational/New Age music. Unfortunately, they withdraw items from their programme, just when I've recommended them, so don't rely on finding what you want. Increasingly, they offer music only in CD form, sometimes even only in double-packs. Still, it's worth sending for their catalogue. The address is: *PO Box 111, East Grinstead, West Sussex, RH19 4FZ. ARC Music products are also available from many record shops.*

Alternatively, ask for advice about suitable music in a record shop or in a shop selling New Age items.

Organisations

The Fellowship of Isis. Clonegal Castle, Enniscorthy, South Ireland. They publish rituals and informative booklets and have a list of ordained priestesses and priests. Please note - all information is available to members only. You can become a member if you like - membership is free. For information, send a stamped addressed envelope or international reply coupon.

The Pagan Federation.BM Box 7097 London WC1N 3XX. The UK's major organisation. They have a list of members who carry out weddings, funerals and other rituals. Enquire with sae.

Please note - both the Fellowship of Isis and the Pagan Federation are sometimes slow to reply and they may need reminders. If you need information urgently, consult other sources as well.

Index

FREE DETAILED CATALOGUE

Capall Bann is owned and run by people actively involved in many of the areas in which we publish. A detailed illustrated catalogue is available on request, SAE or International Postal Coupon appreciated. **Titles can be ordered direct from Capall Bann, post free in the UK** (cheque or PO with order) or from good bookshops and specialist outlets.

Do contact us for details on the latest releases at: **Capall Bann Publishing, Freshfields, Chieveley, Berks, RG20 8TF.** Titles include:

A Breath Behind Time, Terri Hector
Angels and Goddesses - Celtic Christianity & Paganism, M. Howard
Arthur - The Legend Unveiled, C Johnson & E Lung
Astrology The Inner Eye - A Guide in Everyday Language, E Smith
Auguries and Omens - The Magical Lore of Birds, Yvonne Aburrow
Asyniur - Womens Mysteries in the Northern Tradition, S McGrath
Beginnings - Geomancy, Builder's Rites & Electional Astrology Nigel Pennick
Between Earth and Sky, Julia Day
Caer Sidhe - Celtic Astrology and Astronomy, Vol 1, Michael Bayley
Call of the Horned Piper, Nigel Jackson
Cat's Company, Ann Walker
Celtic Faery Shamanism, Catrin James
Celtic Faery Shamanism - The Wisdom of the Otherworld, Catrin James
Celtic Lore & Druidic Ritual, Rhiannon Ryall
Celtic Sacrifice - Pre Christian Ritual & Religion, Marion Pearce
Celtic Saints and the Glastonbury Zodiac, Mary Caine
Circle and the Square, Jack Gale
Compleat Vampyre - The Vampyre Shaman, Nigel Jackson
Creating Form From the Mist - The Wisdom of Women in Celtic Myth and
        Culture, Lynne Sinclair-Wood
Crystal Clear - A Guide to Quartz Crystal, Jennifer Dent
Crystal Doorways, Simon & Sue Lilly
Crossing the Borderlines - Guising, Masking & Ritual Animal Disguise Nigel Pennick
Dragons of the West, Nigel Pennick
Earth Dance - A Year of Pagan Rituals, Jan Brodie
Earth Harmony - Places of Power, Holiness & Healing, Nigel Pennick
Earth Magic, Margaret McArthur
Enchanted Forest - The Magical Lore of Trees, Yvonne Aburrow
Eternal Priestess, Sage Weston
Everything You Always Wanted To Know About Your Body, But So Far
        Nobody's Been Able To Tell You, Chris Thomas & D Baker

Face of the Deep - Healing Body & Soul, Penny Allen
Fairies in the Irish Tradition, Molly Gowen
Familiars - Animal Powers of Britain, Anna Franklin
Fool's First Steps, (The) Chris Thomas
Forest Paths - Tree Divination, Brian Harrison, Ill. S. Rouse
God Year, The, Nigel Pennick & Helen Field
Goddess on the Cross, Dr George Young
Goddess Year, The, Nigel Pennick & Helen Field
Goddesses, Guardians & Groves, Jack Gale
Handbook For Pagan Healers, Liz Joan
Handbook of Fairies, Ronan Coghlan
Healing Book, The, Chris Thomas and Diane Baker
Healing Homes, Jennifer Dent
Healing Stones, Sue Philips
Herb Craft - Shamanic & Ritual Use of Herbs, Lavender & Franklin
In Search of Herne the Hunter, Eric Fitch
Inner Mysteries of the Goths, Nigel Pennick
Inner Space Workbook - Develop Thru Tarot, C Summers & J Vayne
Intuitive Journey, Ann Walker Isis - African Queen, Akkadia Ford
Legend of Robin Hood, The, Richard Rutherford-Moore
Lid Off the Cauldron, Patricia Crowther
Light From the Shadows - Modern Traditional Witchcraft, Gwyn
Magic of Herbs - A Complete Home Herbal, Rhiannon Ryall
Magical Guardians - Exploring the Spirit and Nature of Trees, Philip Heselton
Magical History of the Horse, Janet Farrar & Virginia Russell
Magical Lore of Animals, Yvonne Aburrow
Magical Lore of Cats, Marion Davies
Magical Lore of Herbs, Marion Davies
Magick Without Peers, Ariadne Rainbird & David Rankine
Masks of Misrule - Horned God & His Cult in Europe, Nigel Jackson
Medicine For The Coming Age, Lisa Sand MD
Medium Rare - Reminiscences of a Clairvoyant, Muriel Renard
Mind Massage - 60 Creative Visualisations, Marlene Maundrill
Moon Mysteries, Jan Brodie
Mysteries of the Runes, Michael Howard
Mystic Life of Animals, Ann Walker
Pagan Feasts - Seasonal Food for the 8 Festivals, Franklin & Phillips
Patchwork of Magic - Living in a Pagan World, Julia Day
Pathworking - A Practical Book of Guided Meditations, Pete Jennings
Personal Power, Anna Franklin
Pickingill Papers - The Origins of Gardnerian Wicca, Bill Liddell
Practical Meditation, Steve Hounsome
Practical Spirituality, Steve Hounsome
Psychic Self Defence - Real Solutions, Jan Brodie
Real Fairies, David Tame
Romany Tapestry, Michael Houghton

Runic Astrology, Nigel Pennick
Sacred Animals, Gordon MacLellan
Sacred Celtic Animals, Marion Davies, Ill. Simon Rouse
Sacred Dorset - On the Path of the Dragon, Peter Knight
Sacred Grove - The Mysteries of the Forest, Yvonne Aburrow
Sacred Geometry, Nigel Pennick
Sacred Nature, Ancient Wisdom & Modern Meanings, A Cooper
Sacred Ring - Pagan Origins of British Folk Festivals, M. Howard
Season of Sorcery - On Becoming a Wisewoman, Poppy Palin
Seasonal Magic - Diary of a Village Witch, Paddy Slade
Secret Places of the Goddess, Philip Heselton
Spirits of the Air, Jaq D Hawkins
Spirits of the Earth, Jaq D Hawkins
Spirits of the Earth, Jaq D Hawkins
Stony Gaze, Investigating Celtic Heads John Billingsley
Stumbling Through the Undergrowth , Mark Kirwan-Heyhoe
Subterranean Kingdom, The, revised 2nd ed, Nigel Pennick
Symbols of Ancient Gods, Rhiannon Ryall
Talking to the Earth, Gordon MacLellan
Taming the Wolf - Full Moon Meditations, Steve Hounsome
Teachings of the Wisewomen, Rhiannon Ryall
The Other Kingdoms Speak, Helena Hawley
Tree: Essence of Healing, Simon & Sue Lilly
Tree: Essence, Spirit & Teacher, Simon & Sue Lilly
Understanding Chaos Magic, Jaq D Hawkins
Warp and Weft - In Search of the I-Ching, William de Fancourt
Warriors at the Edge of Time, Jan Fry
Water Witches, Tony Steele
Way of the Magus, Michael Howard
West Country Wicca, Rhiannon Ryall
Wildwitch - The Craft of the Natural Psychic, Poppy Palin
Wildwood King , Philip Kane
Witches of Oz, Matthew & Julia Philips
Wondrous Land - The Faery Faith of Ireland by Dr Kay Mullin
Working With the Merlin, Geoff Hughes
Your Talking Pet, Ann Walker

FREE detailed catalogue and FREE 'Inspiration' magazine

Contact: Capall Bann Publishing, Freshfields, Chieveley, Berks, RG20 8TF